Larissa's Adult Coloring Book

By Larissa Suter

Color Pallet

Color Pallet

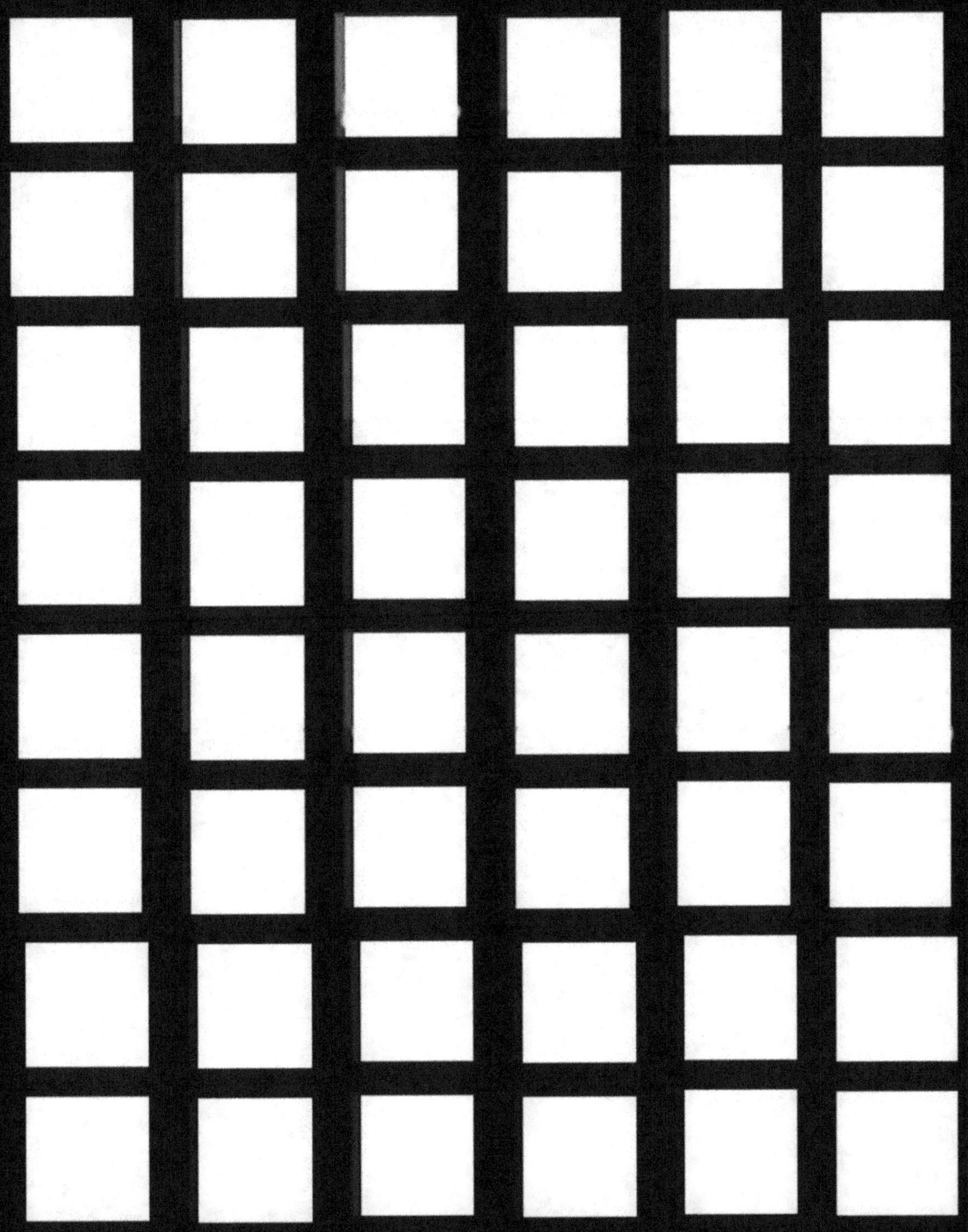

Color Pallet

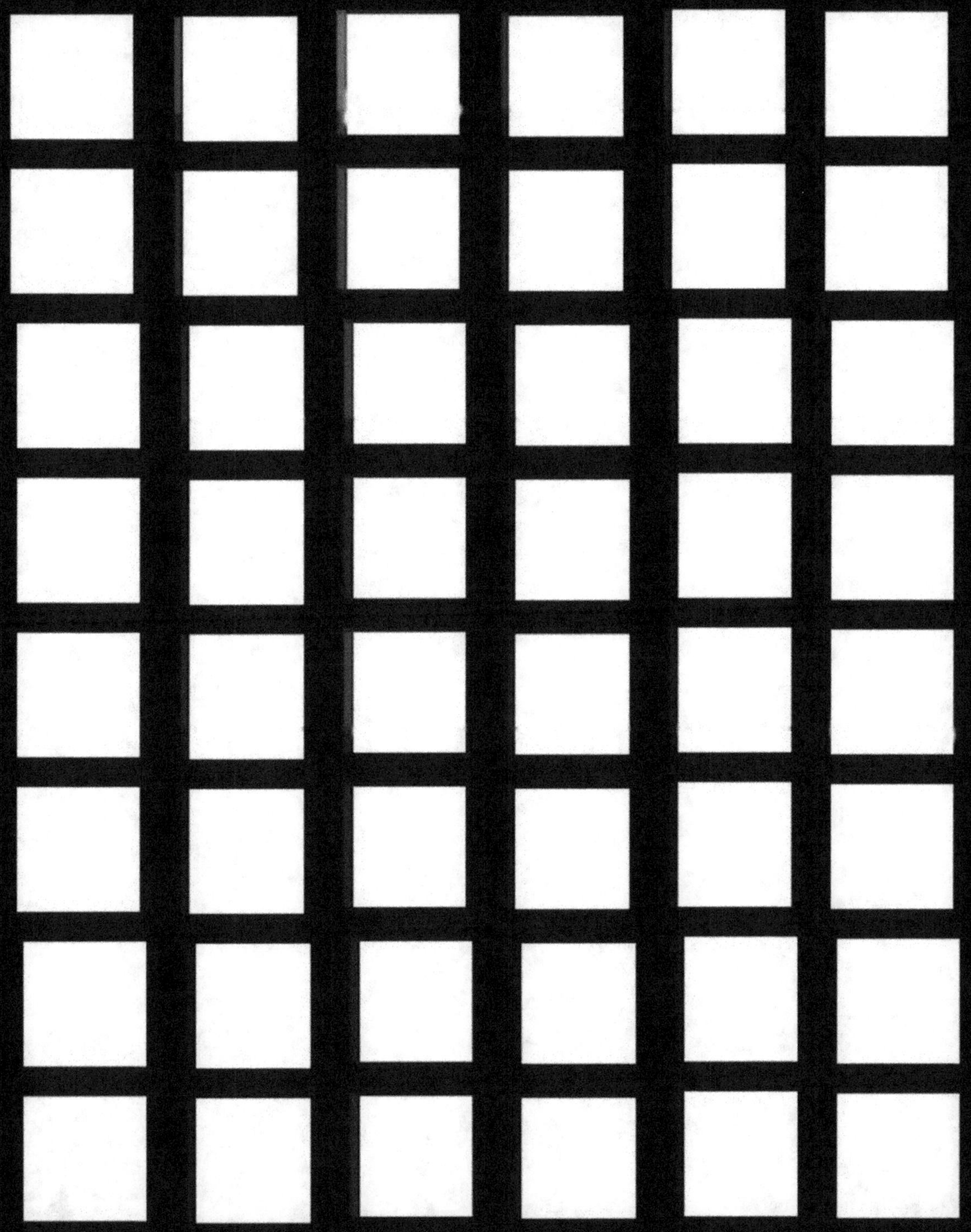

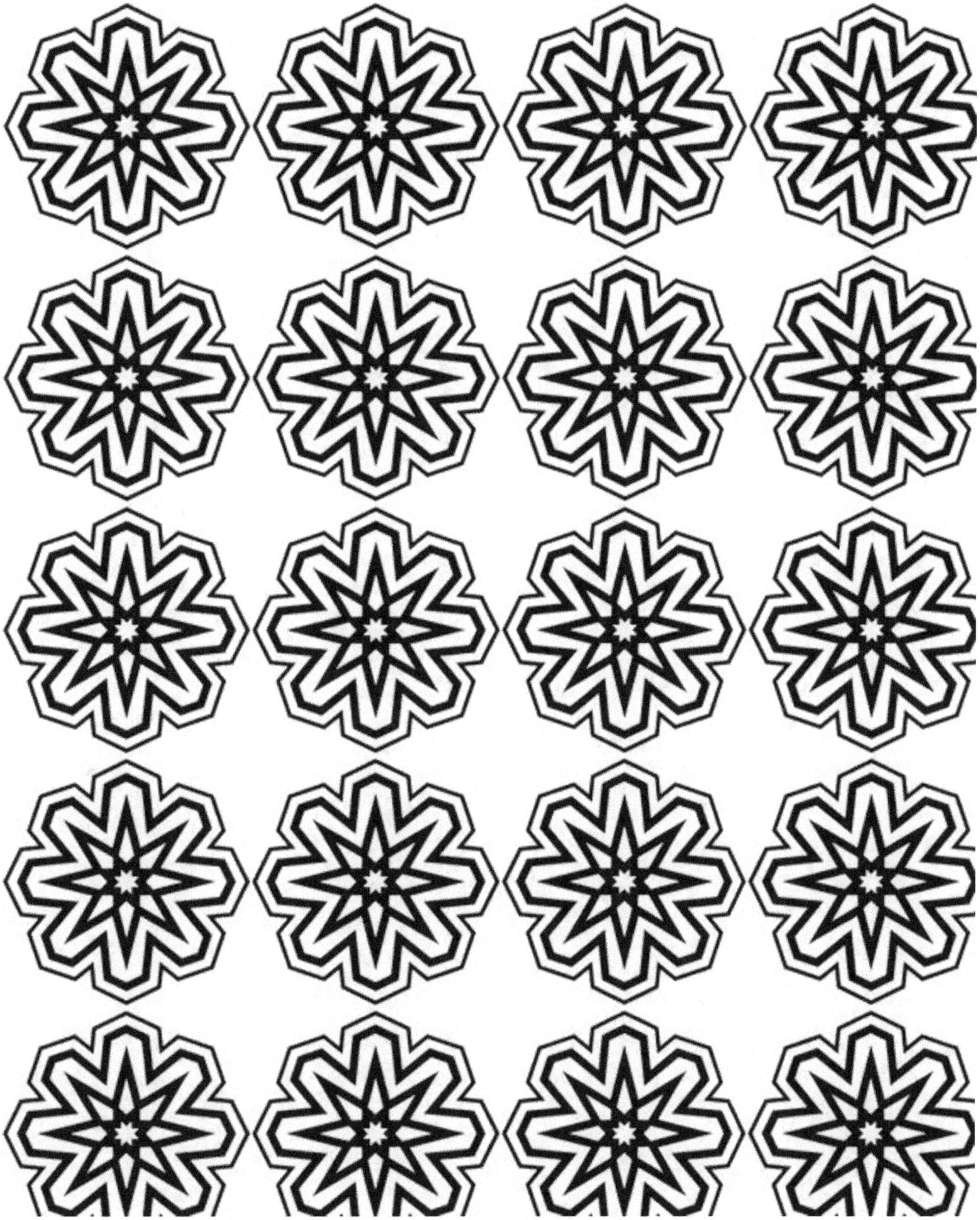

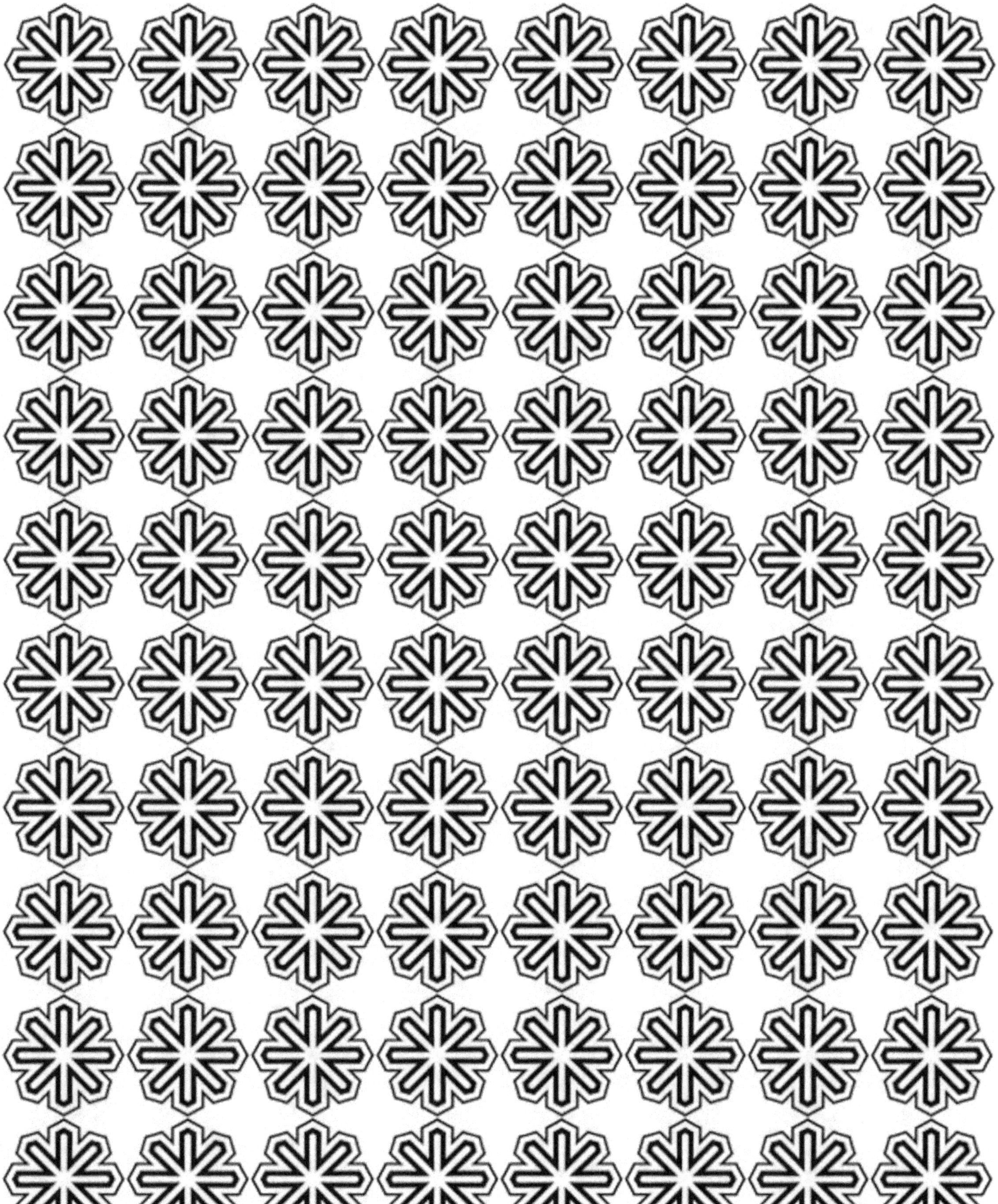

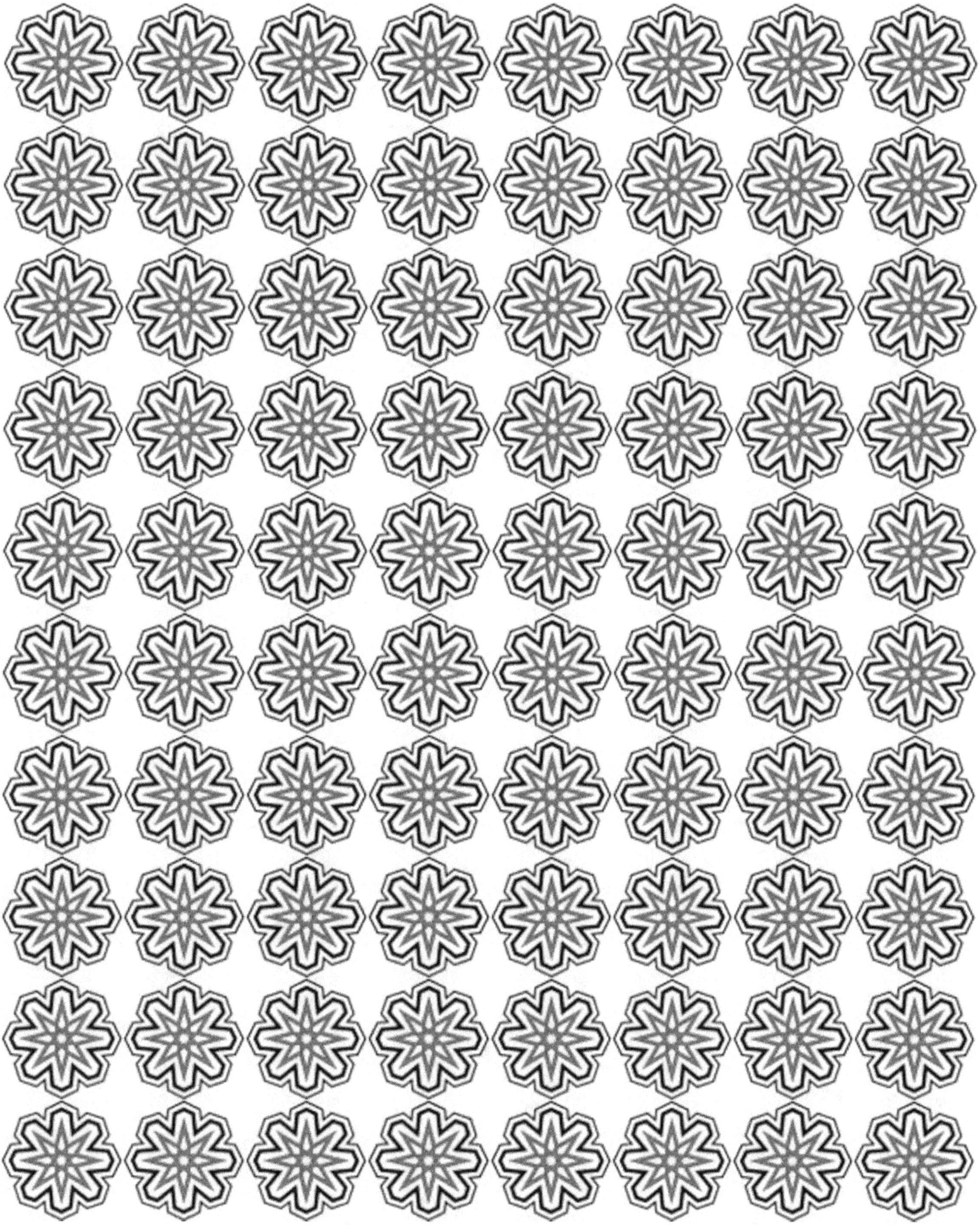

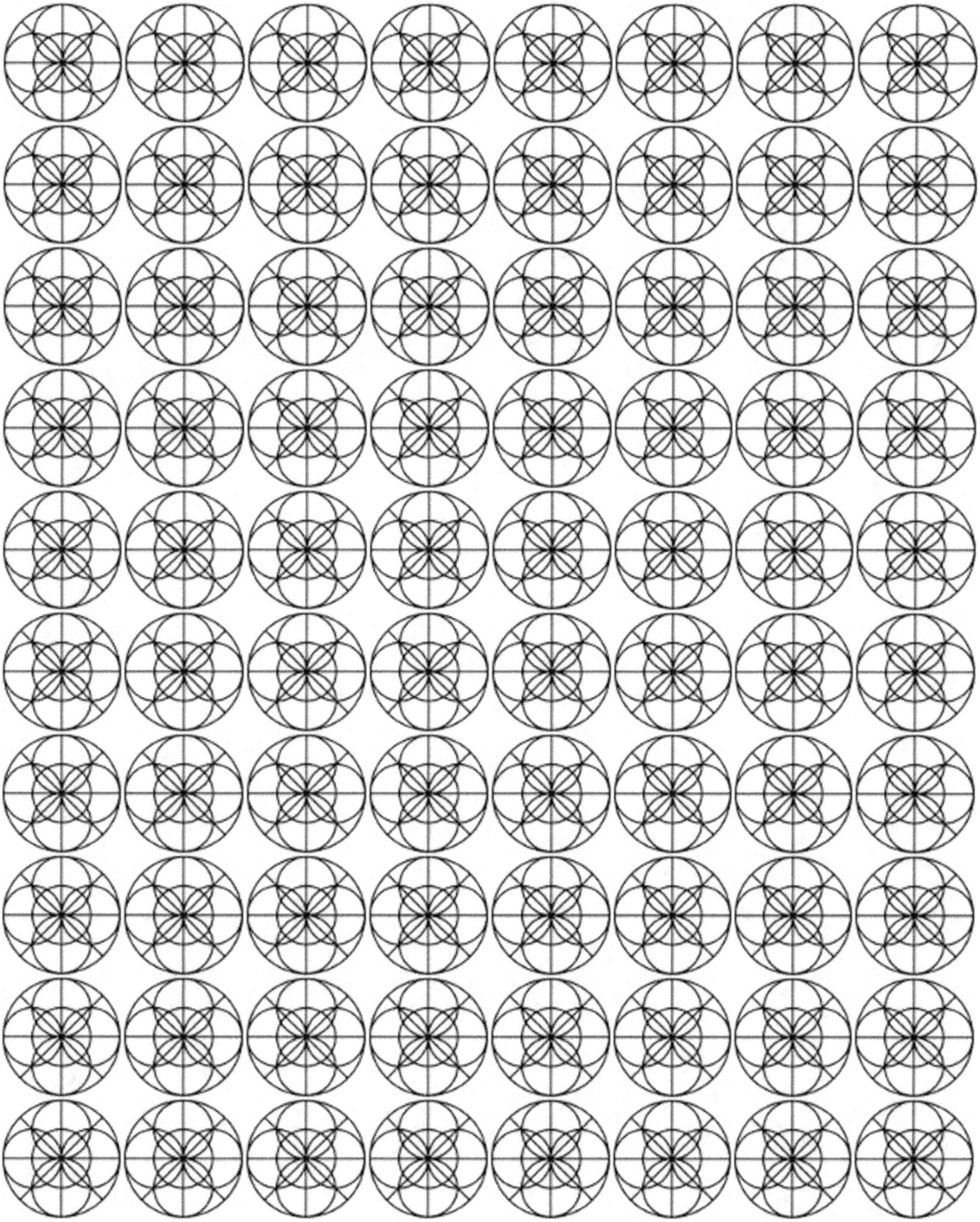

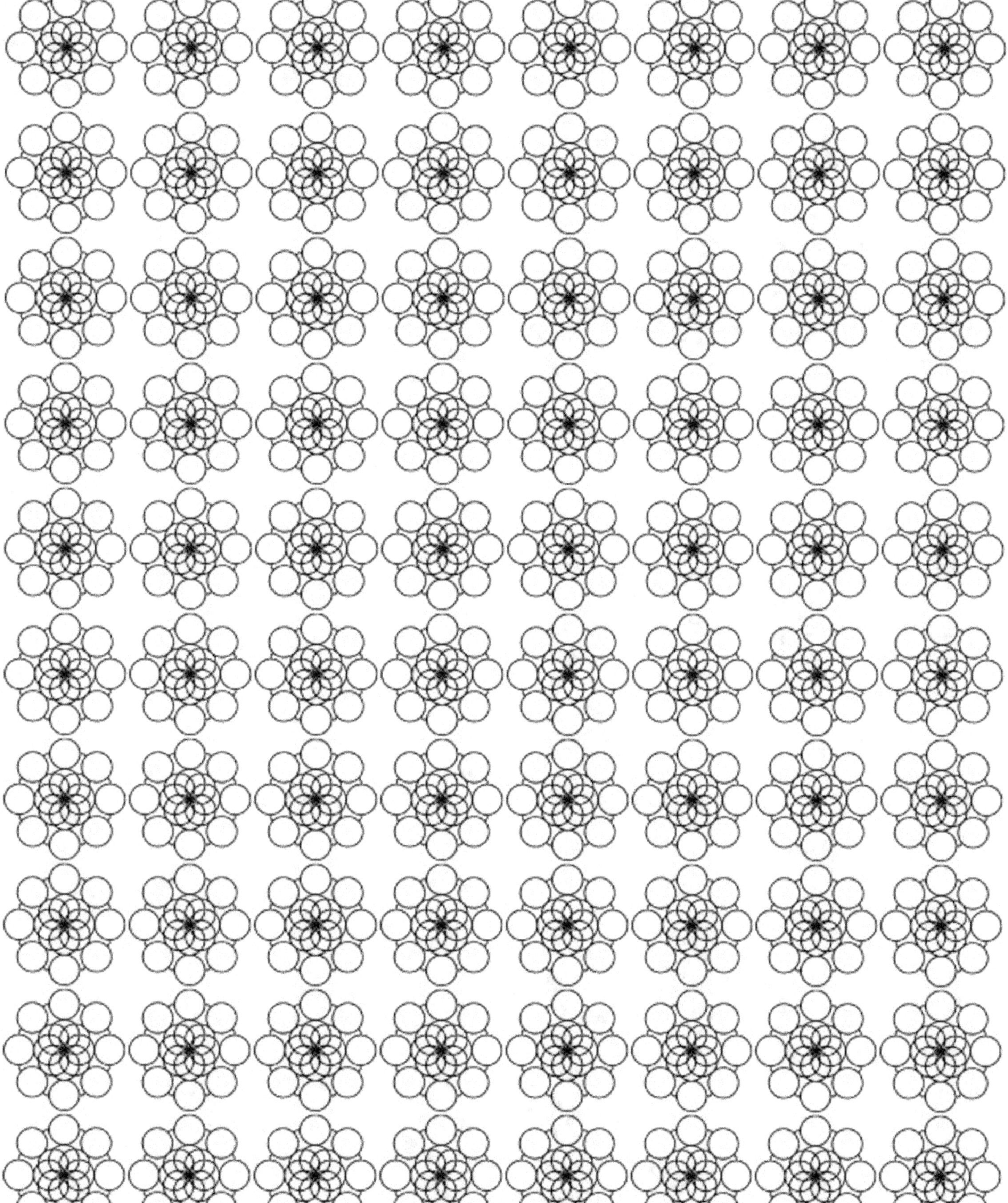

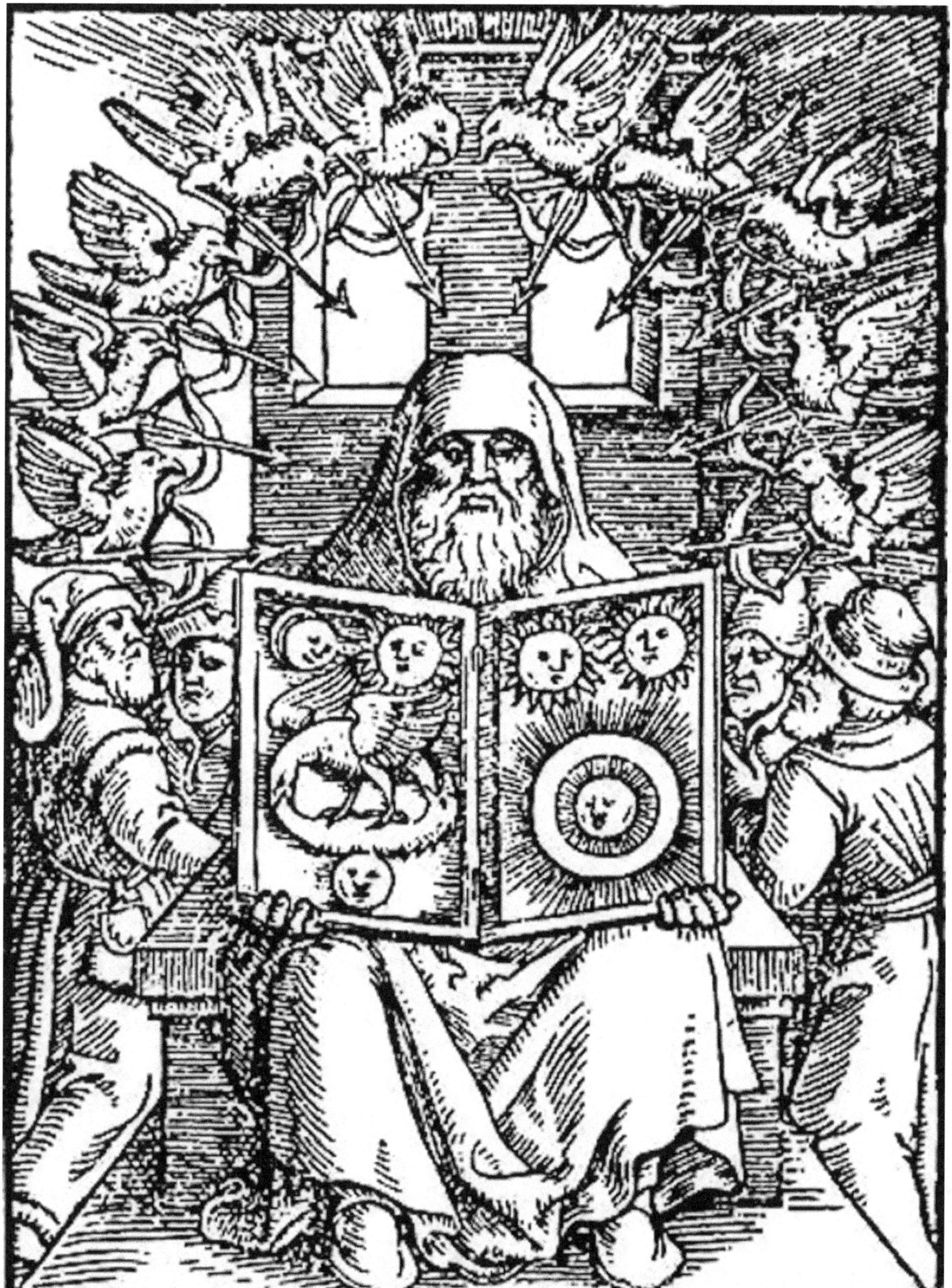

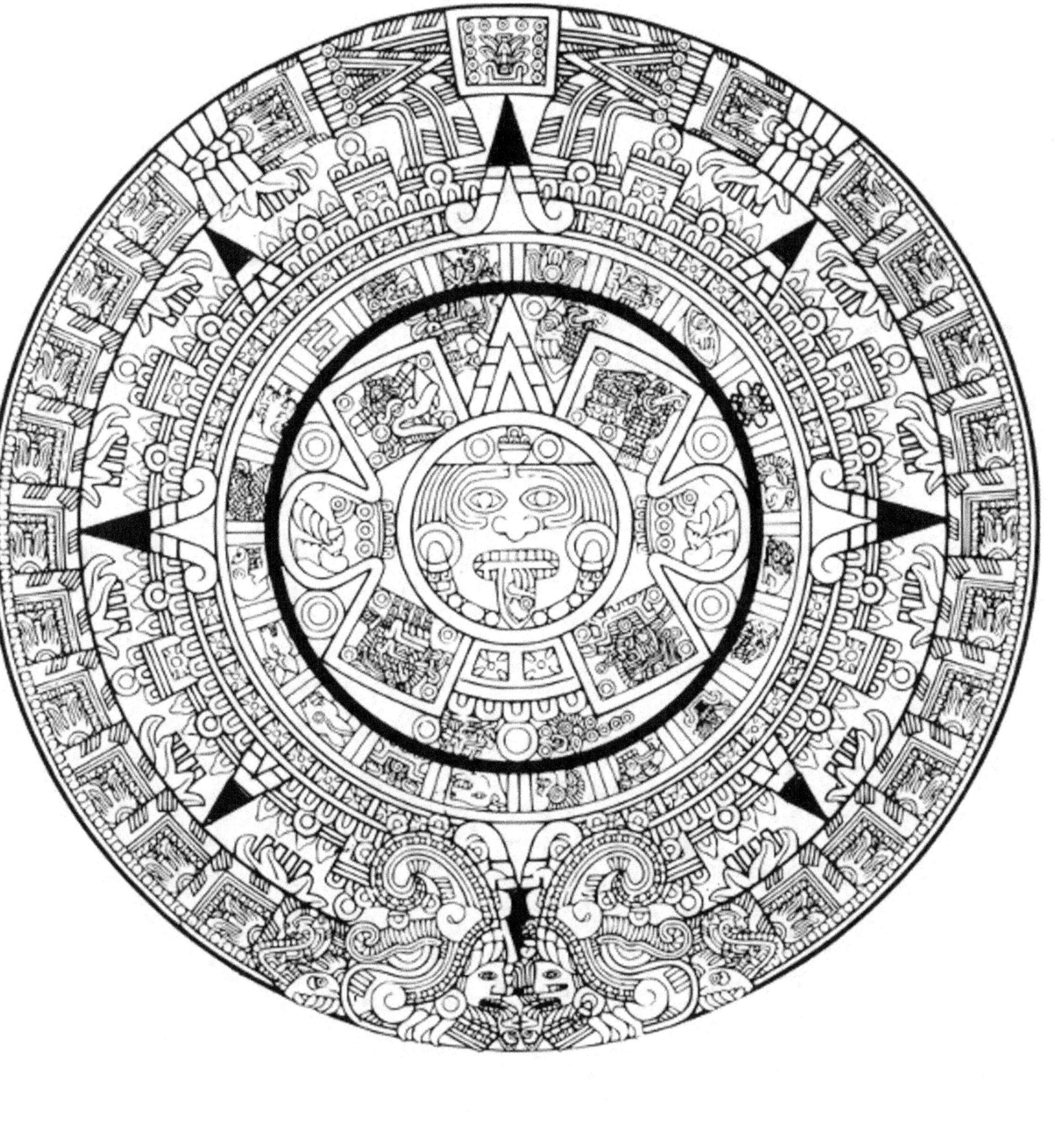

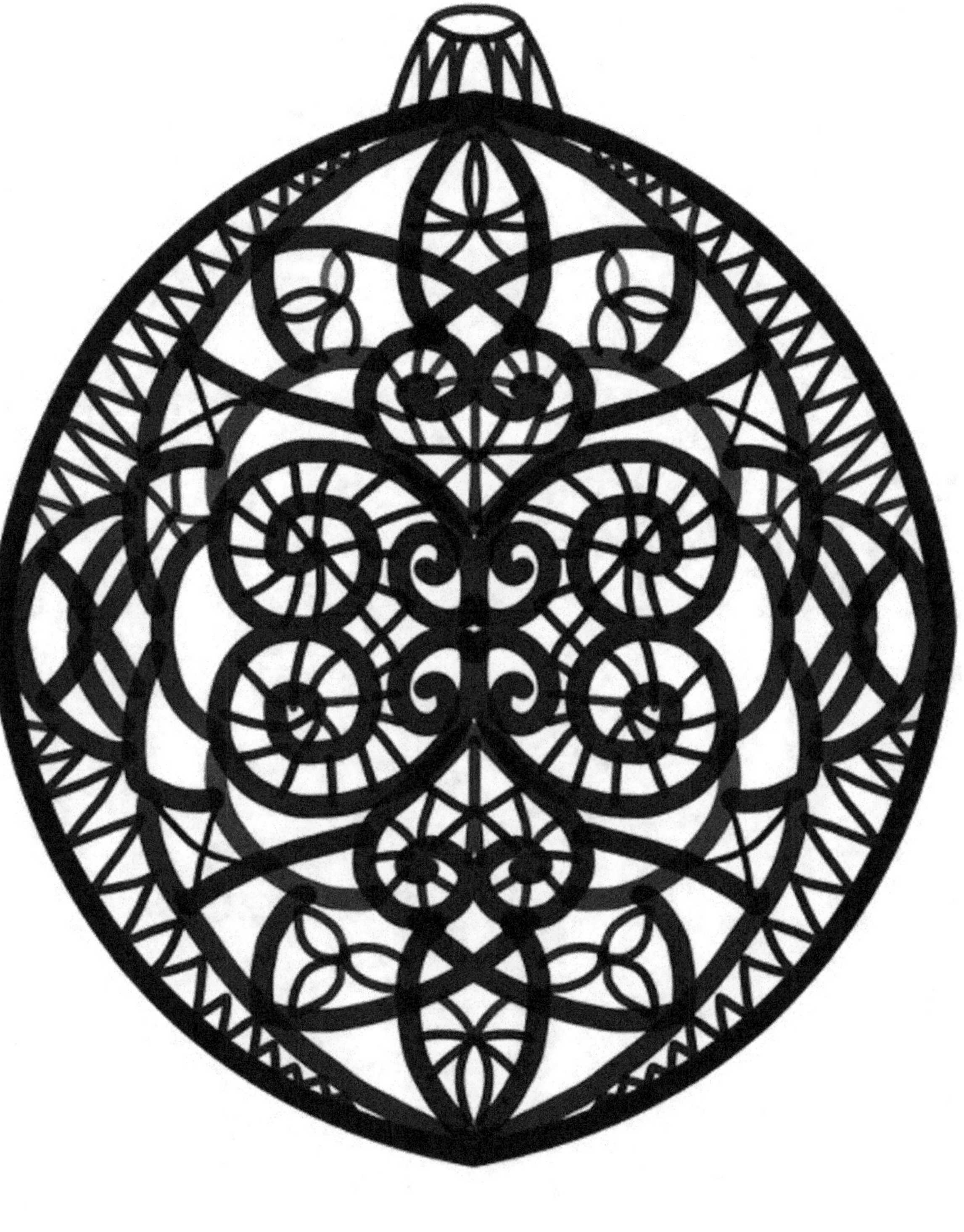

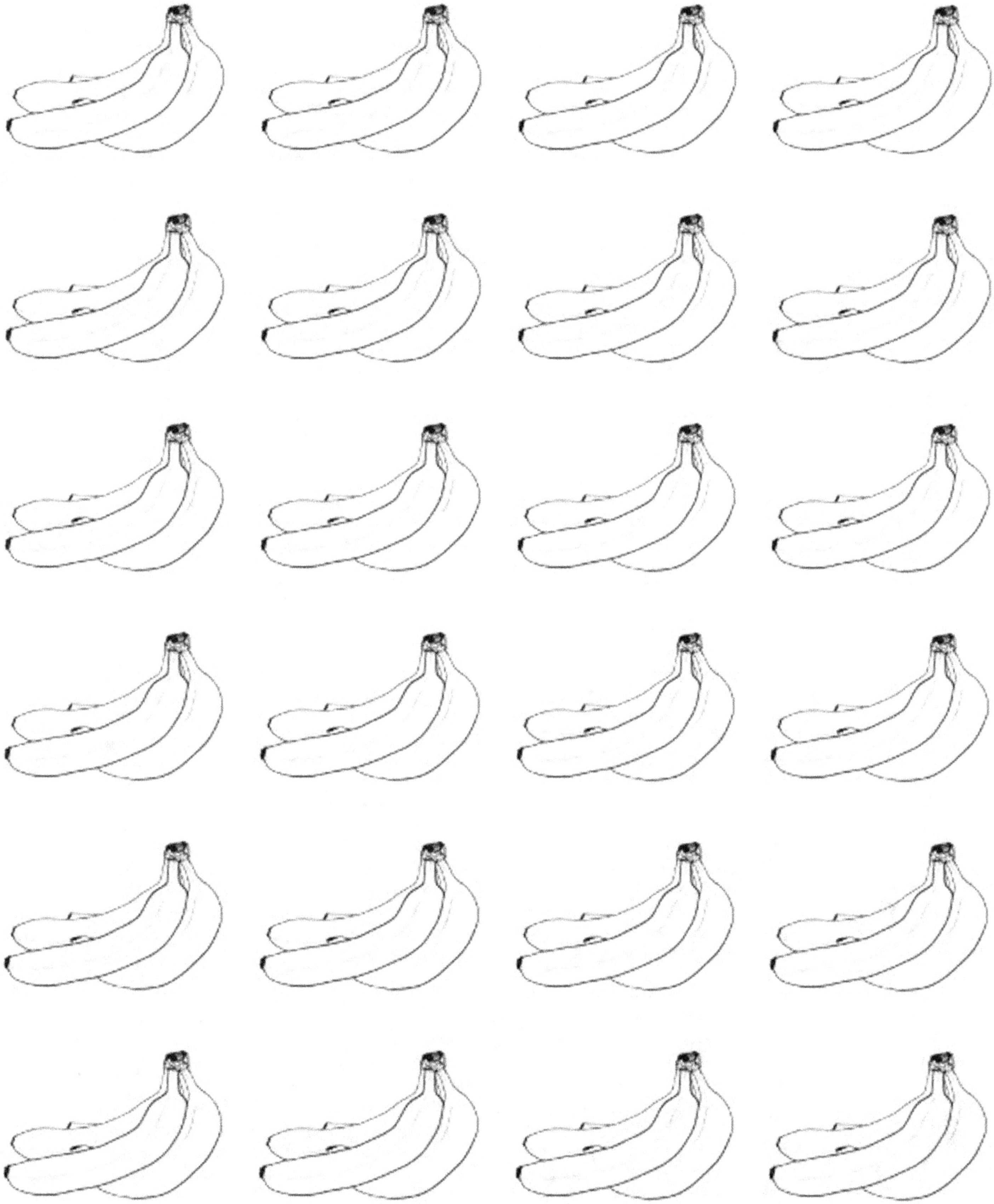

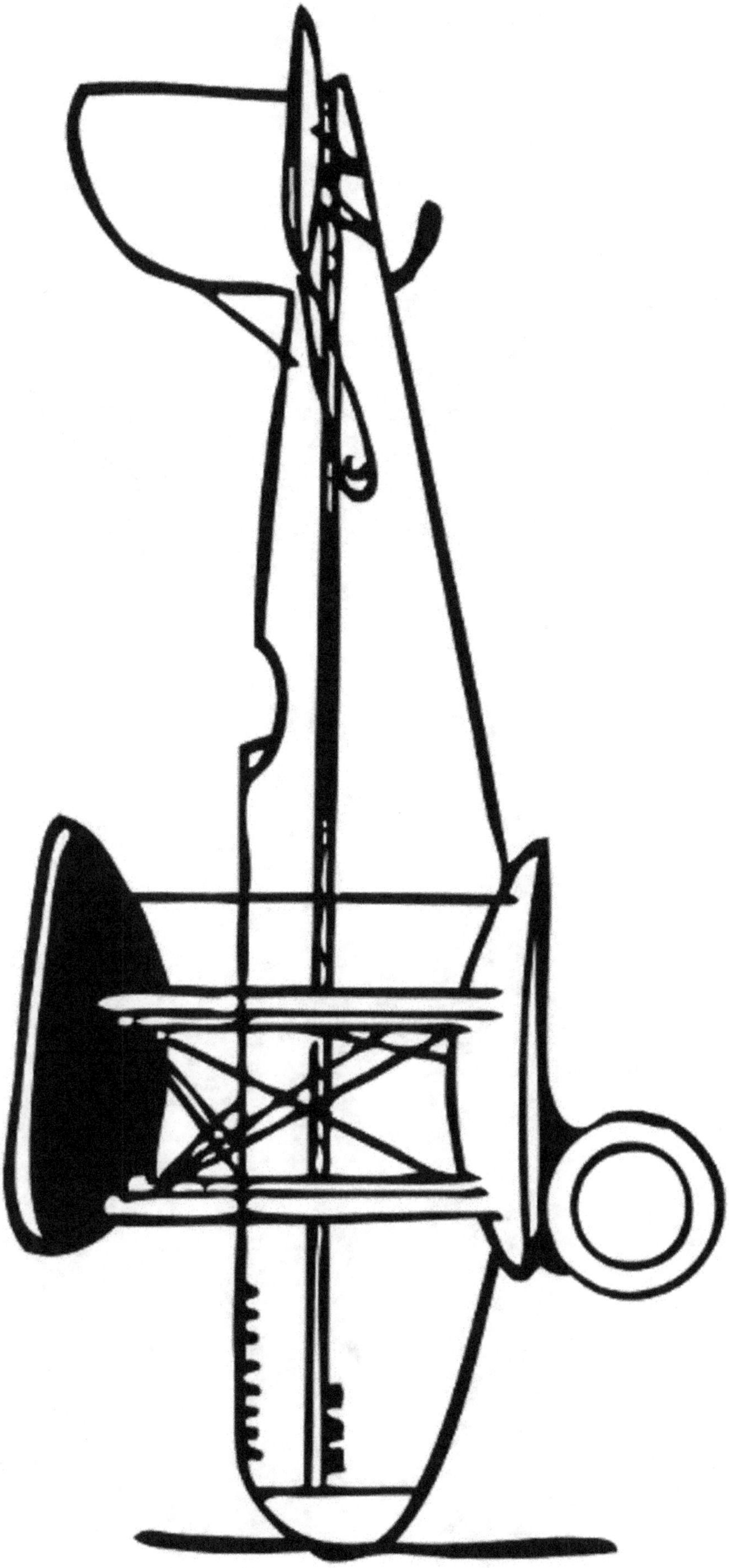

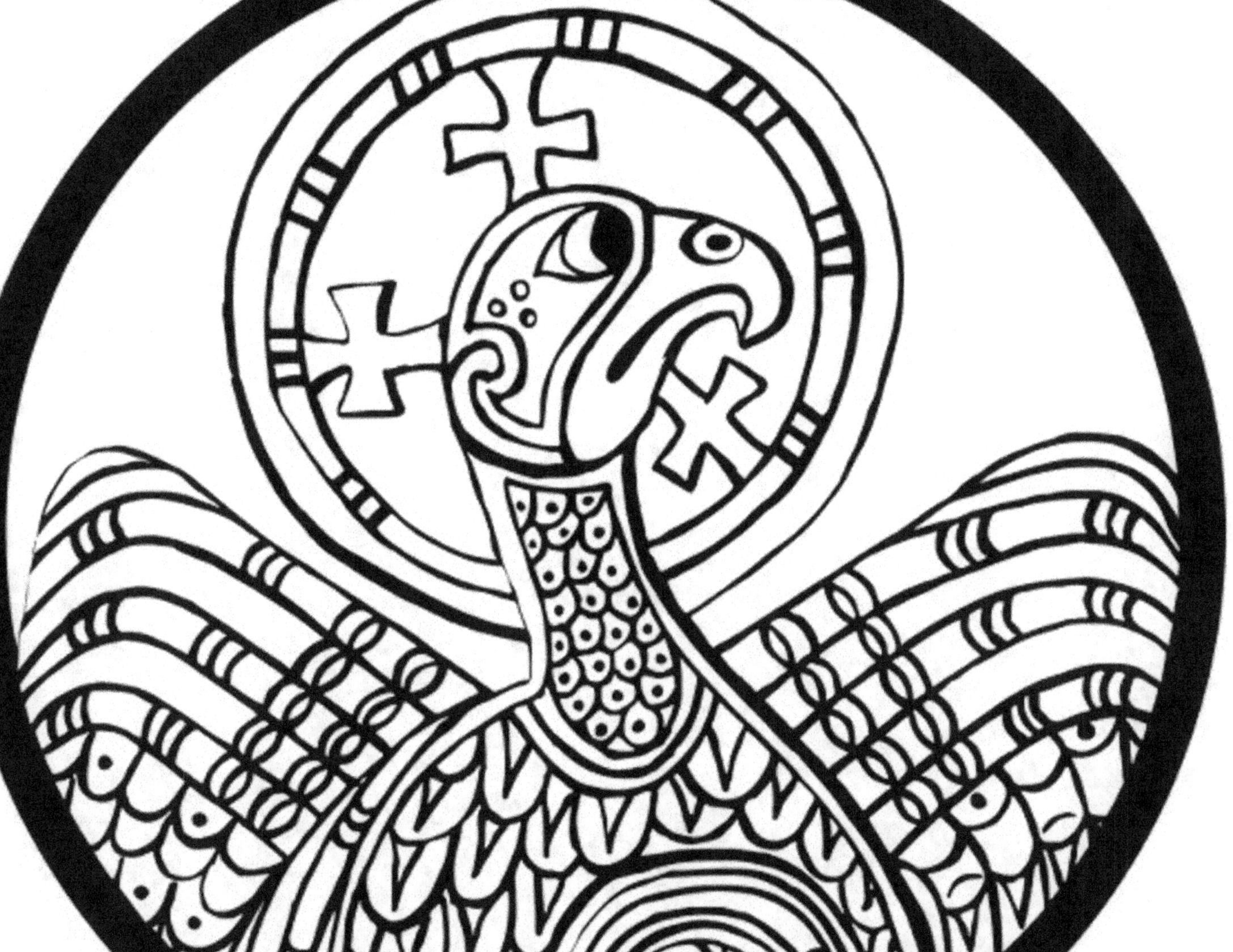

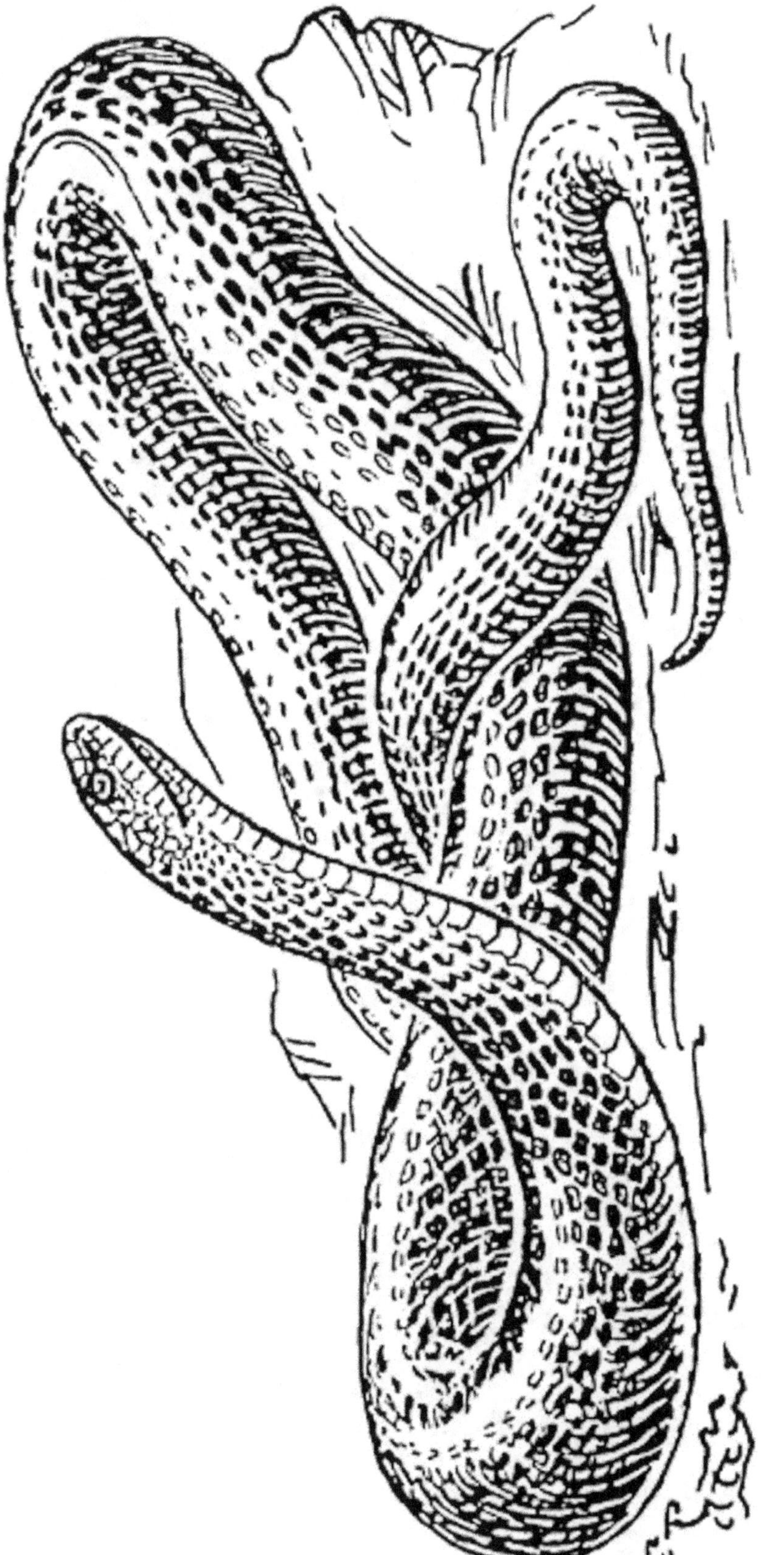

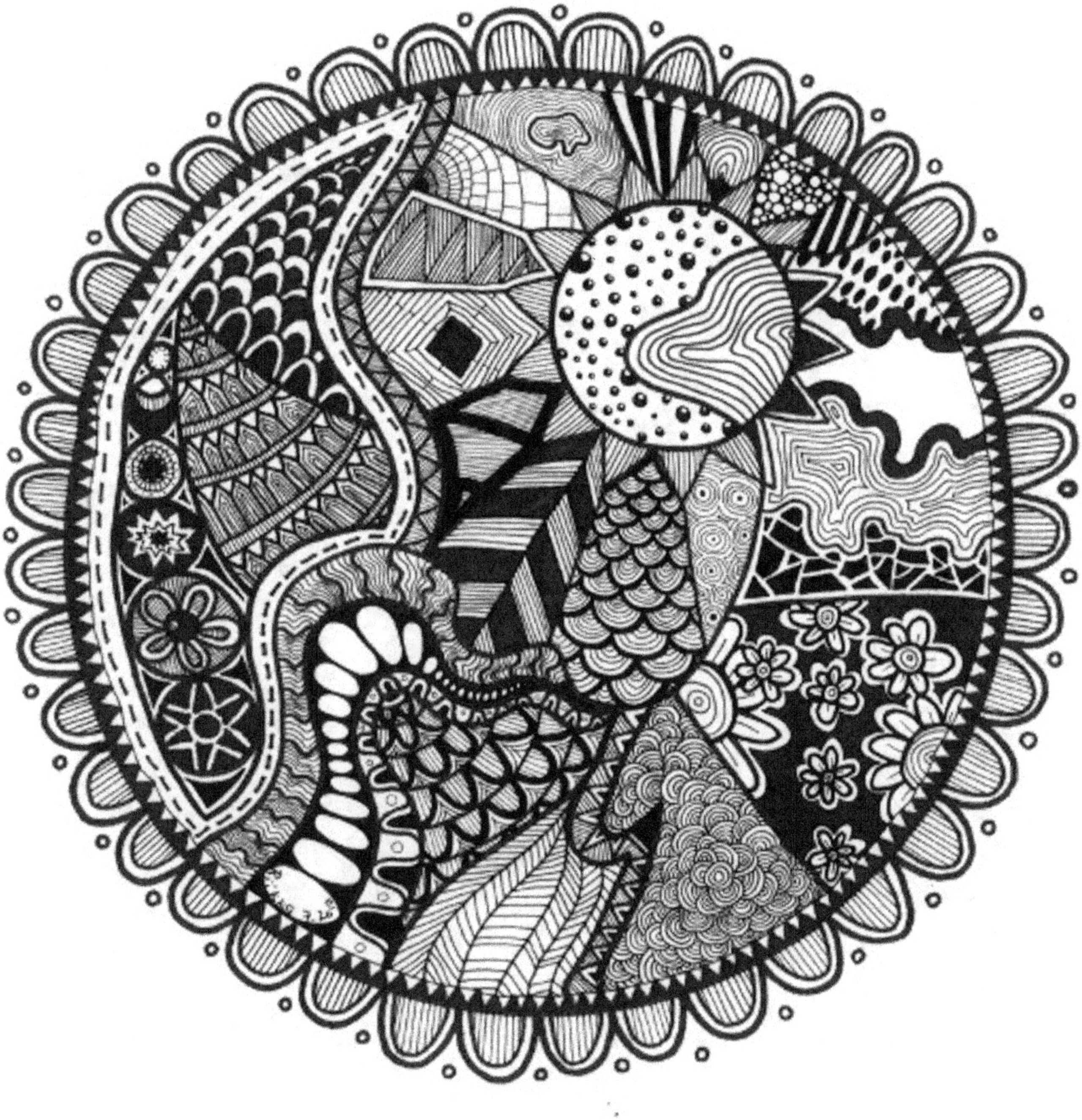

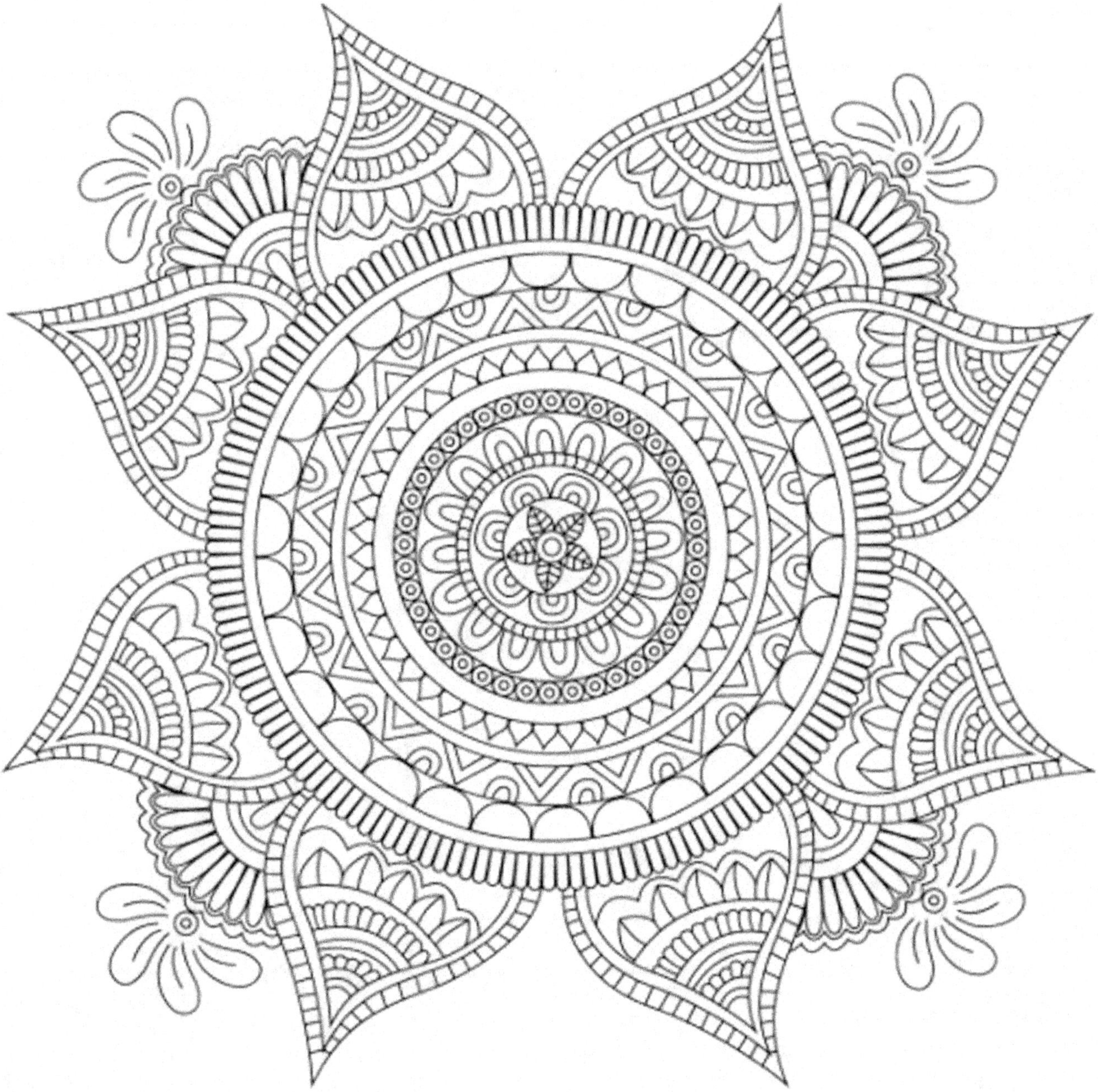

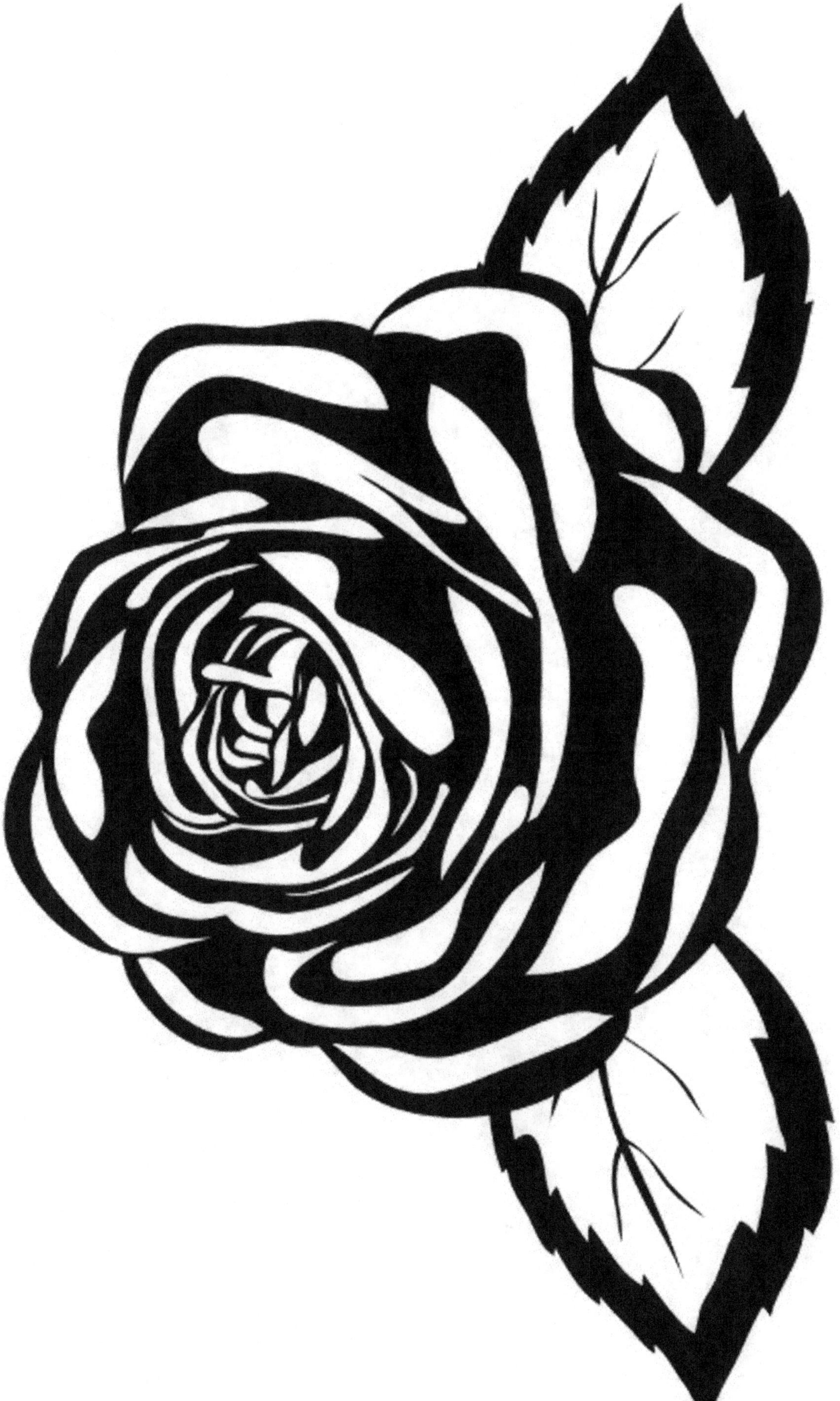

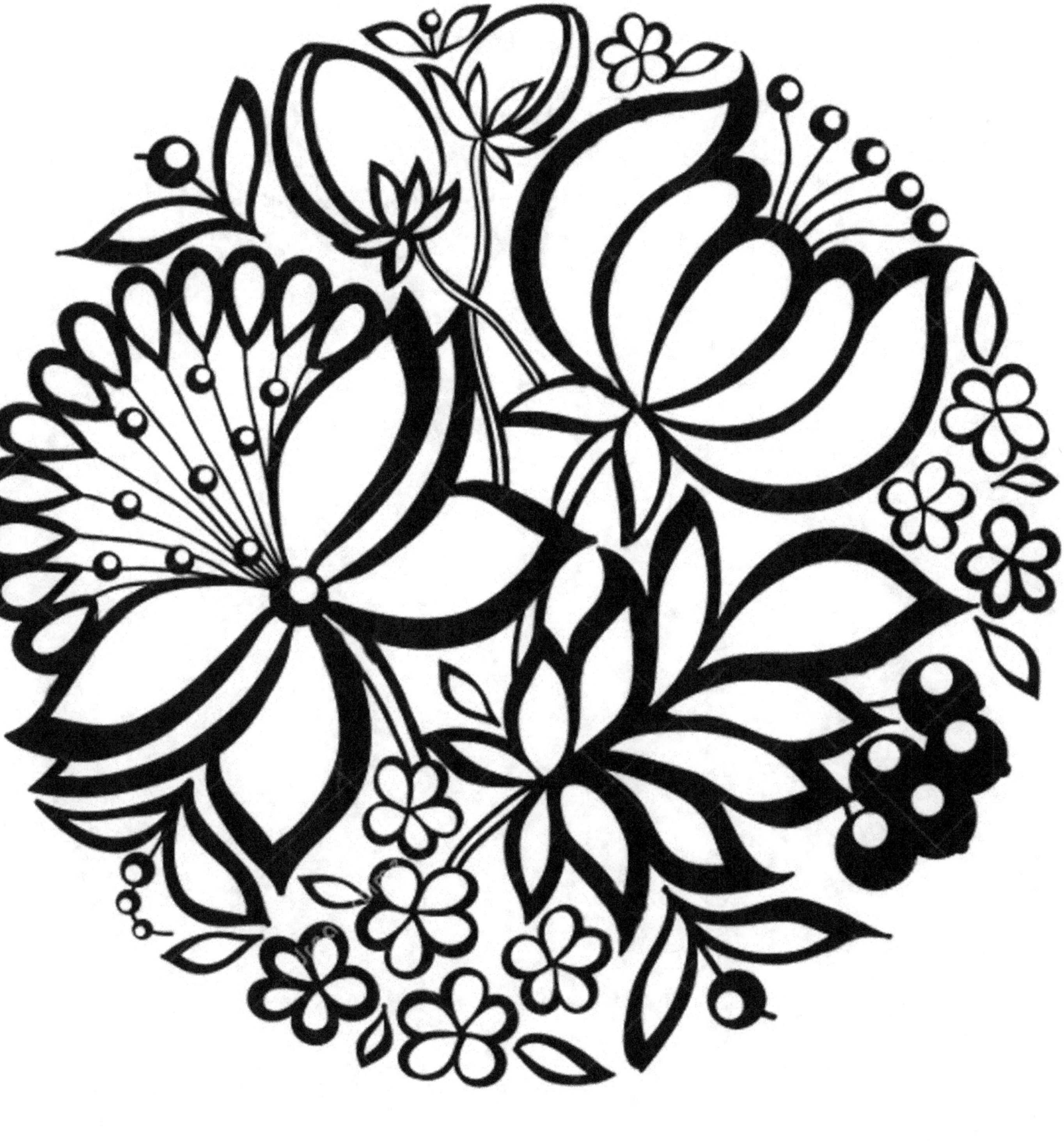

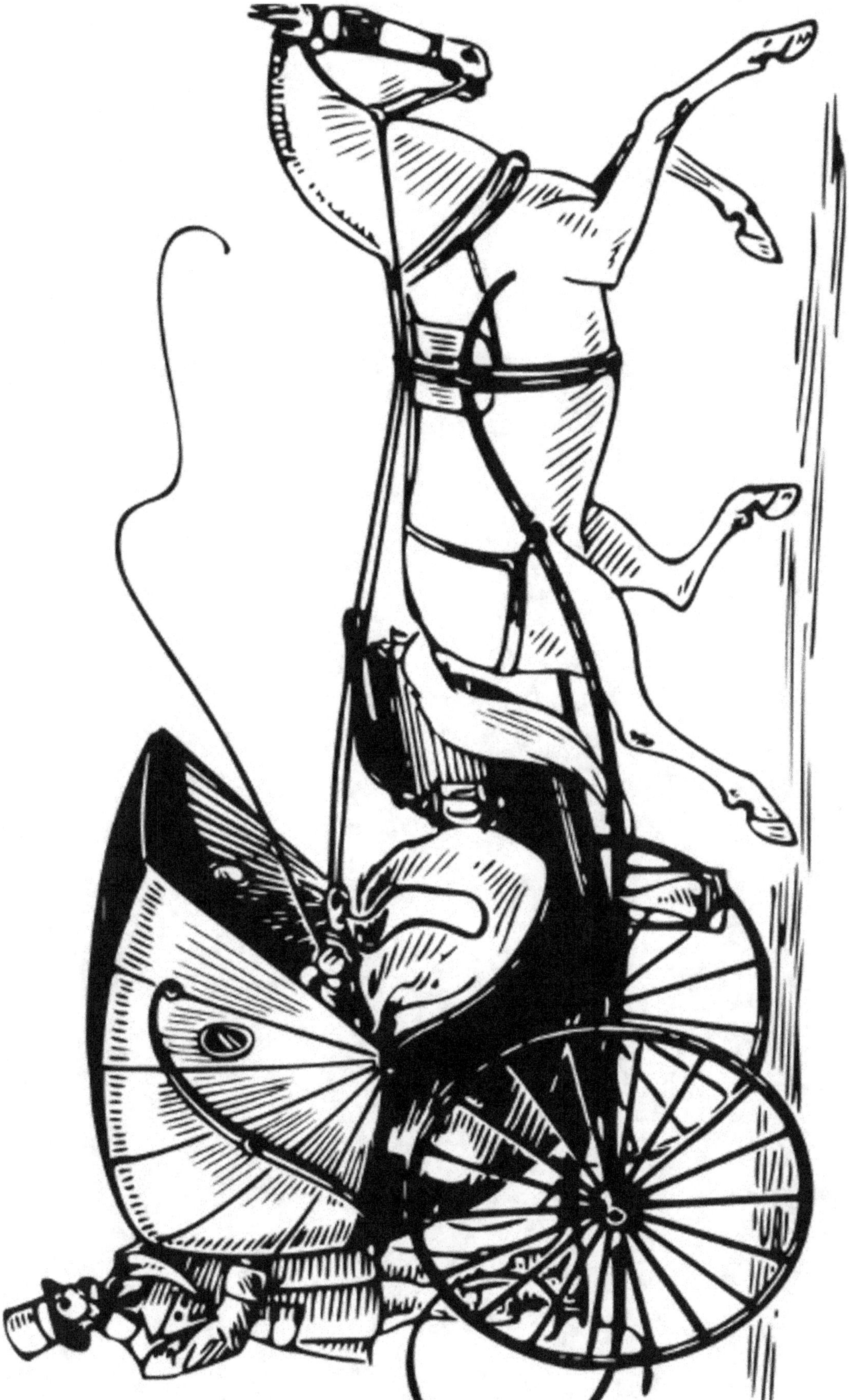

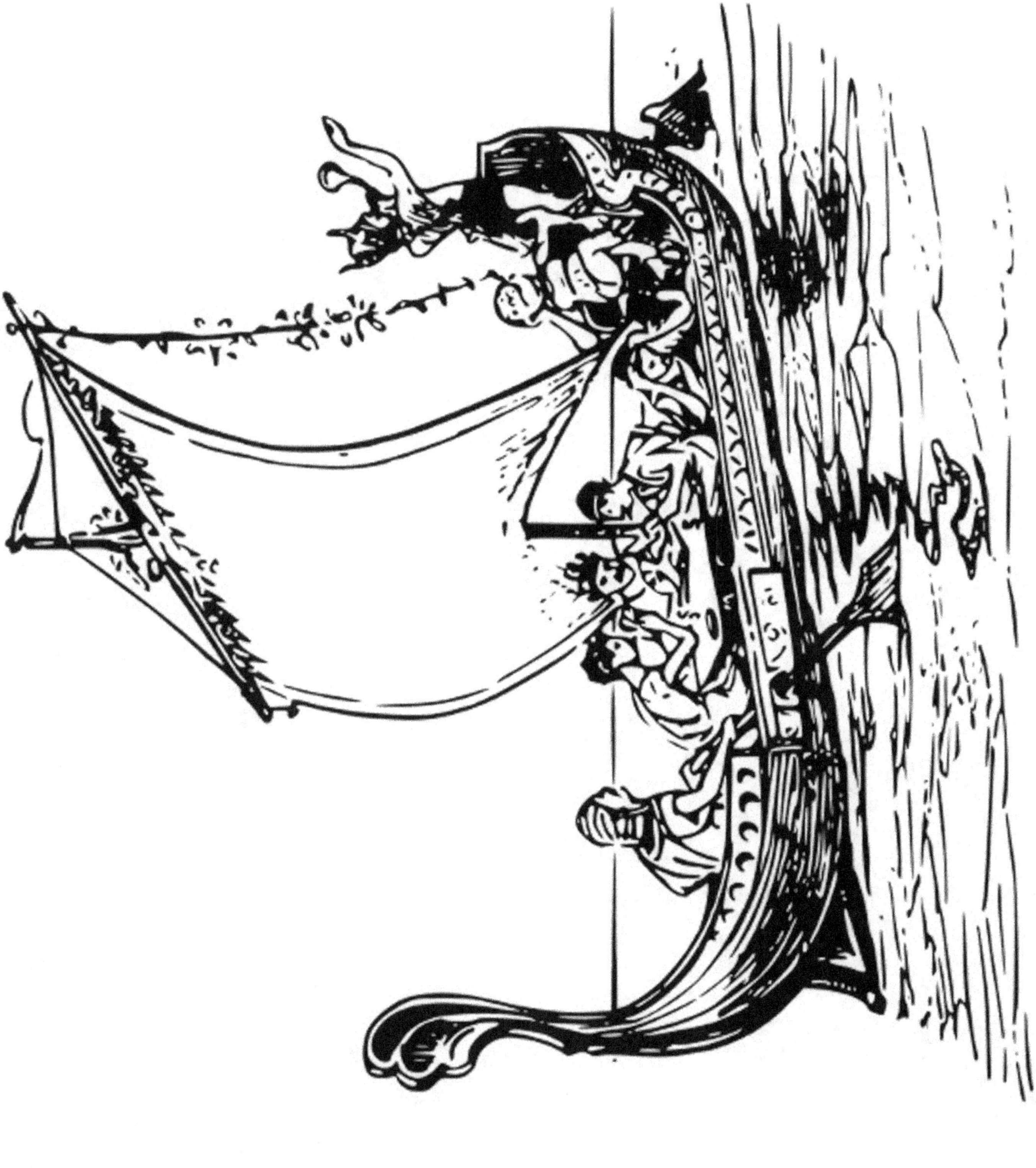

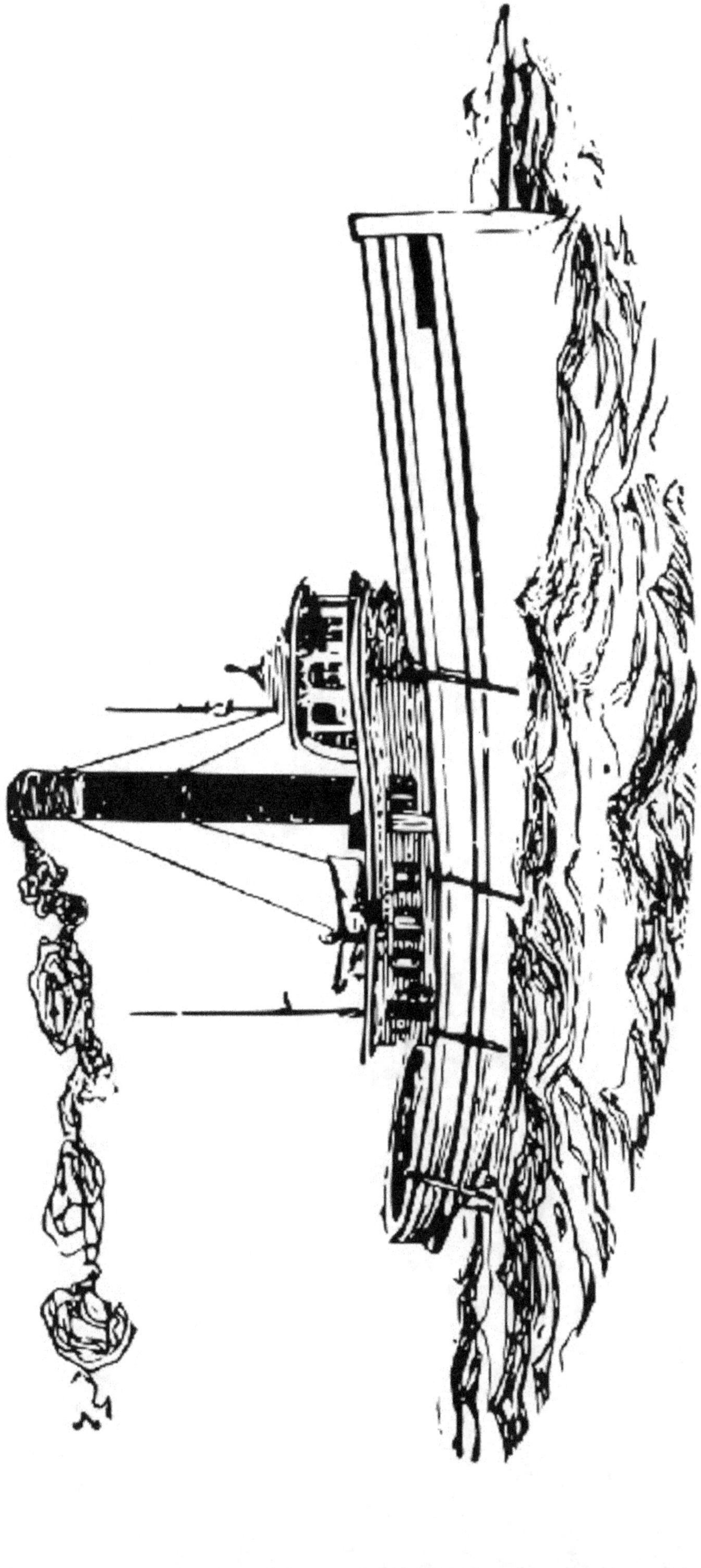

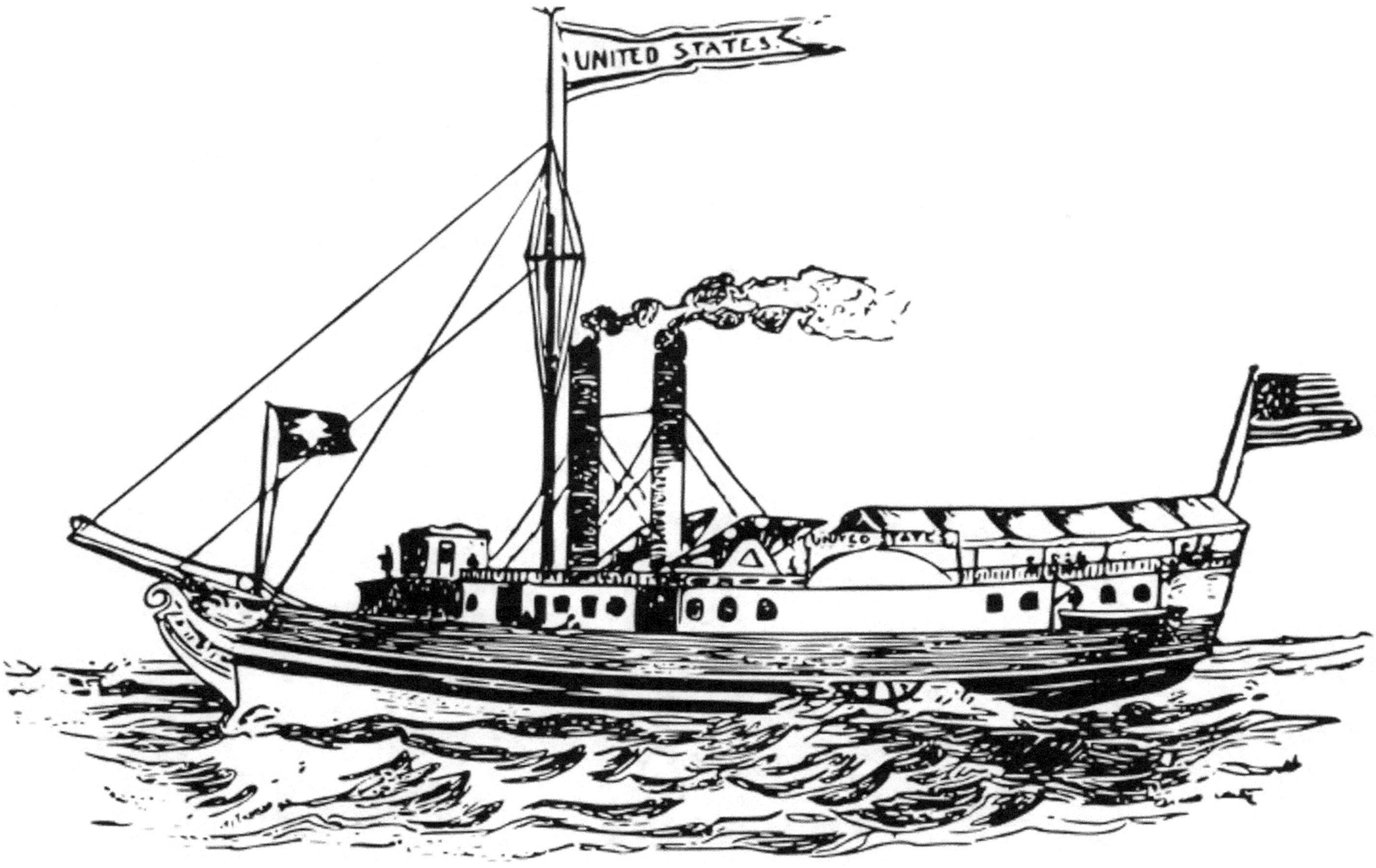
UNITED STATES

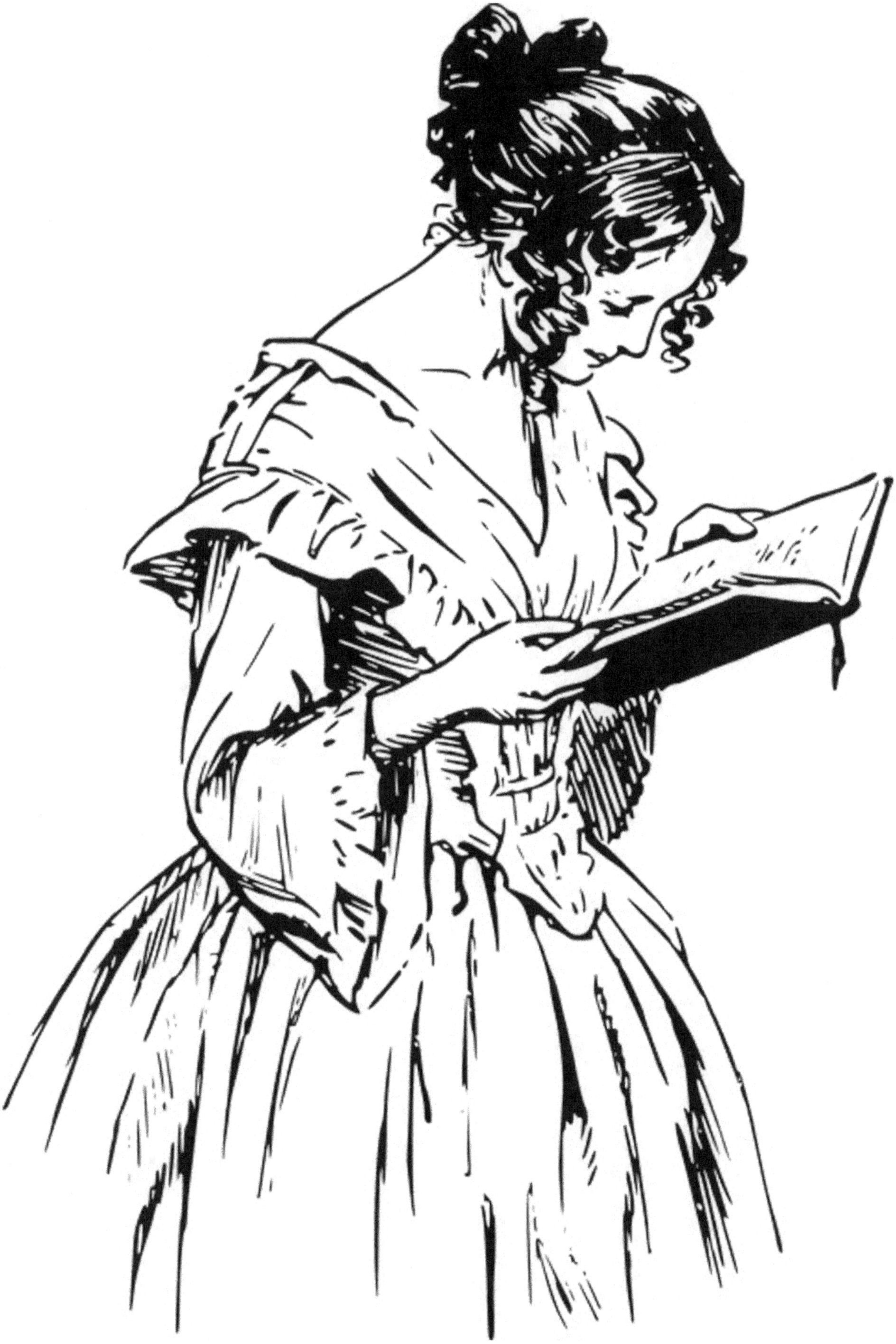

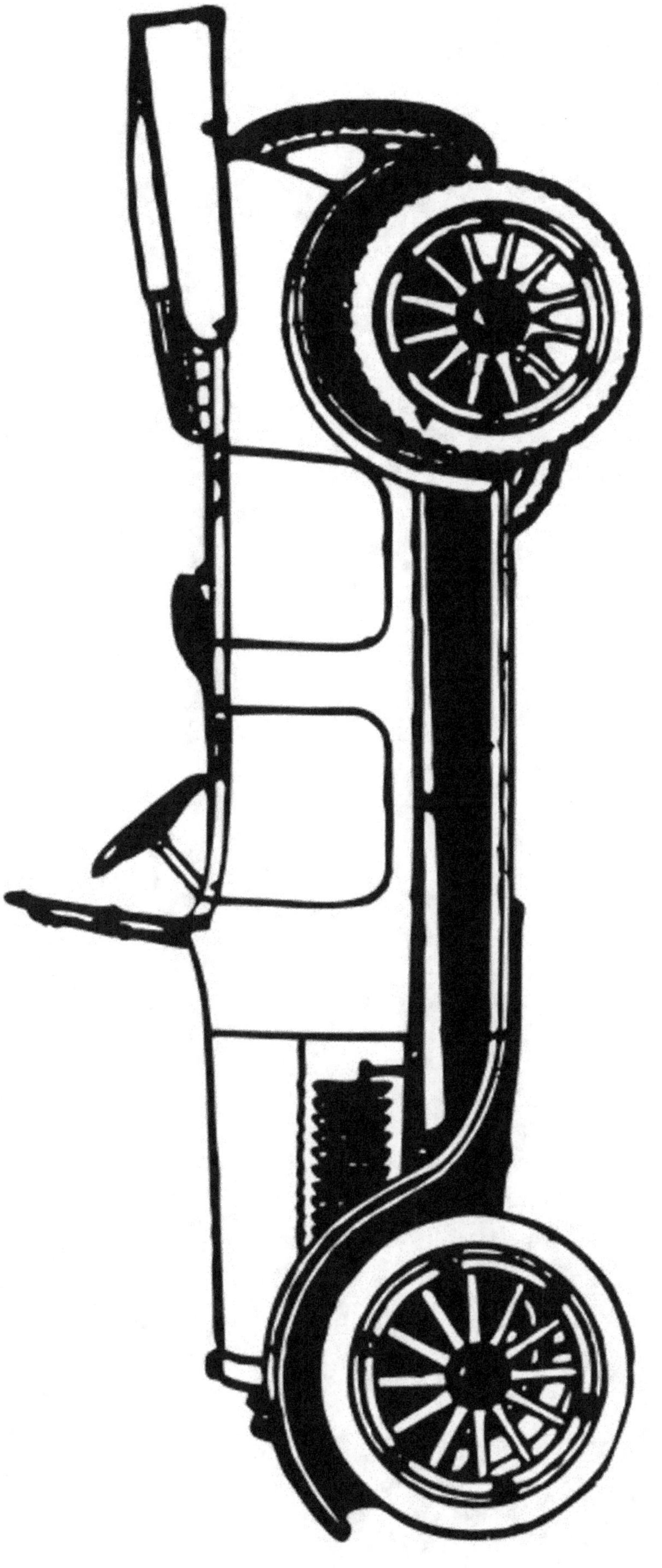

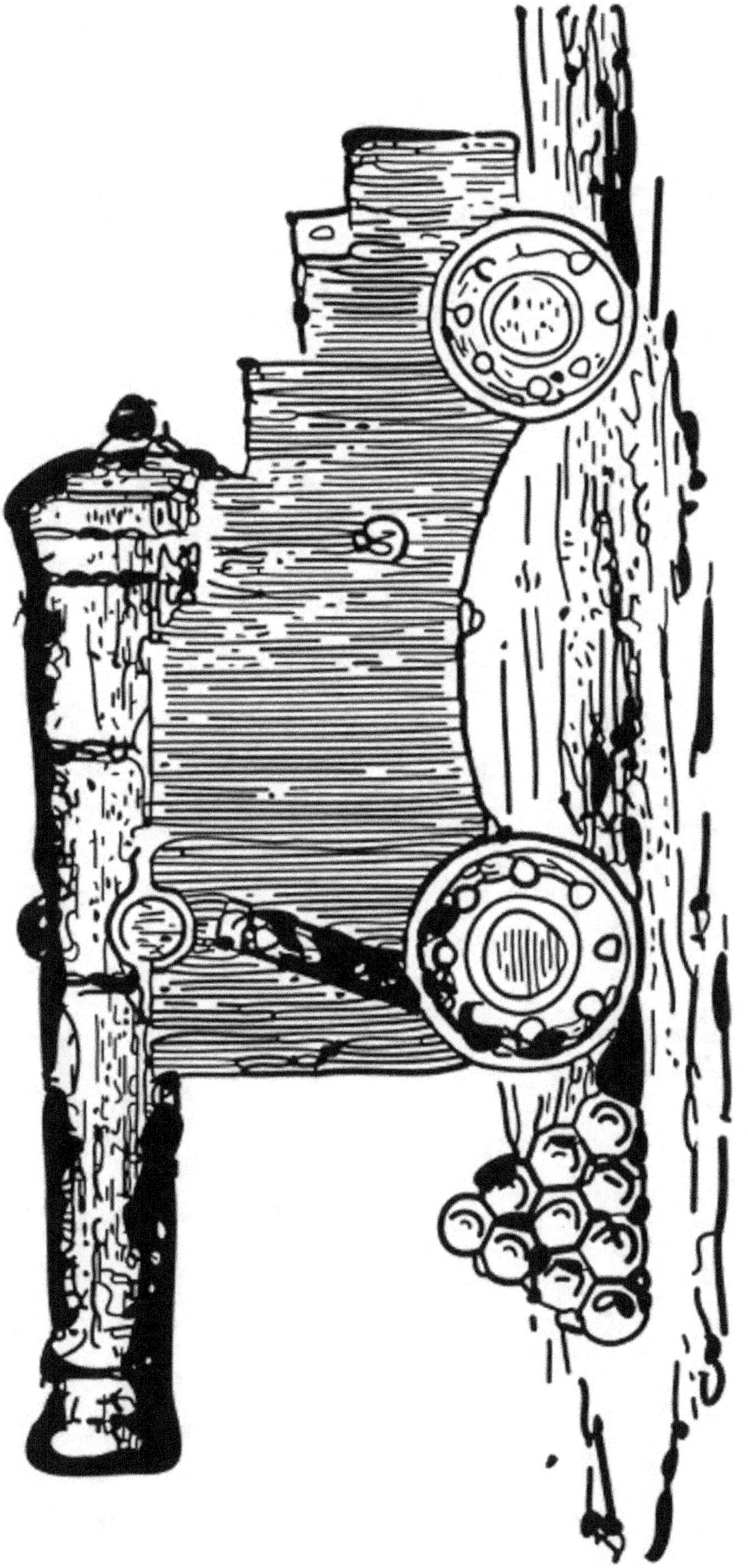

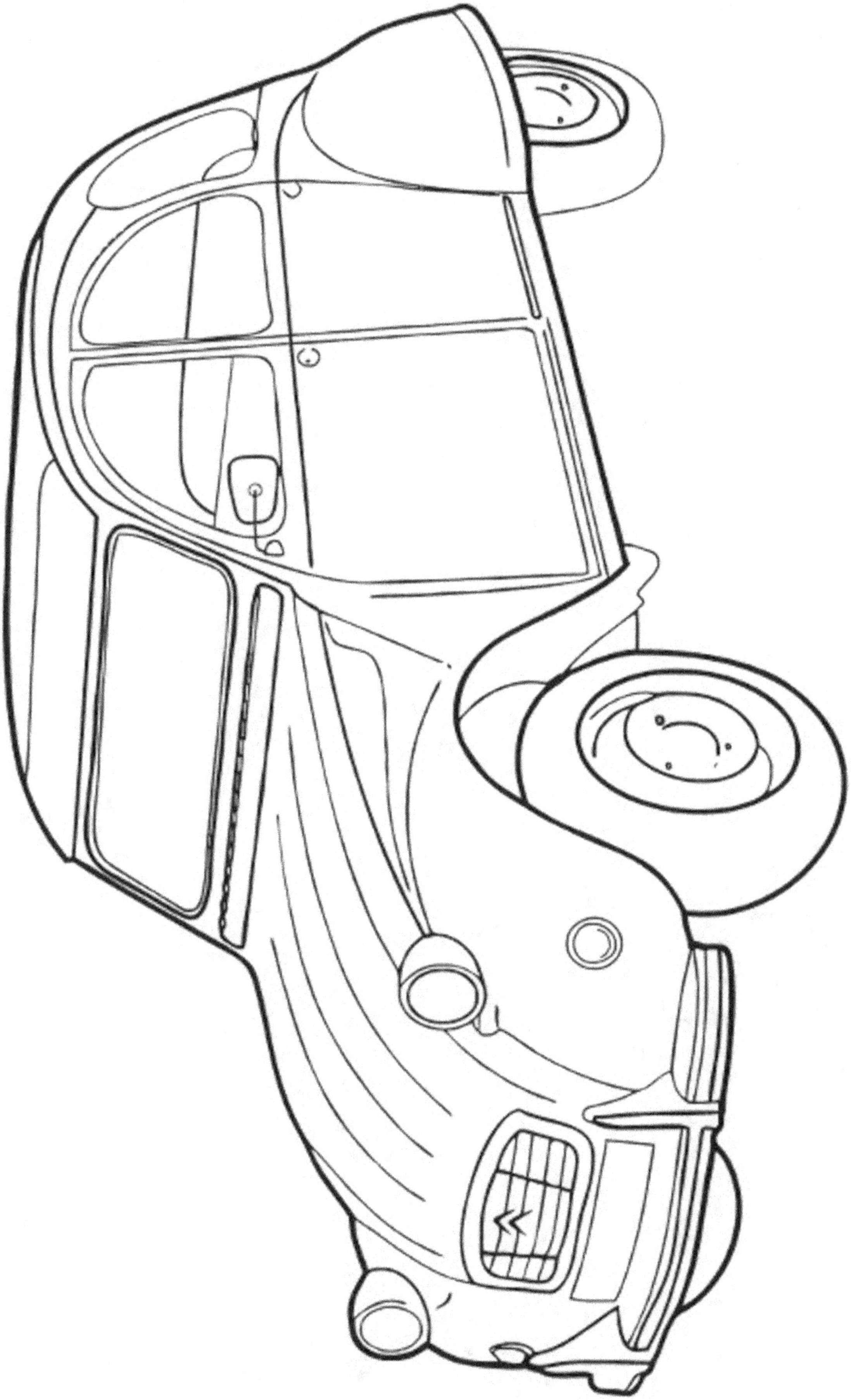

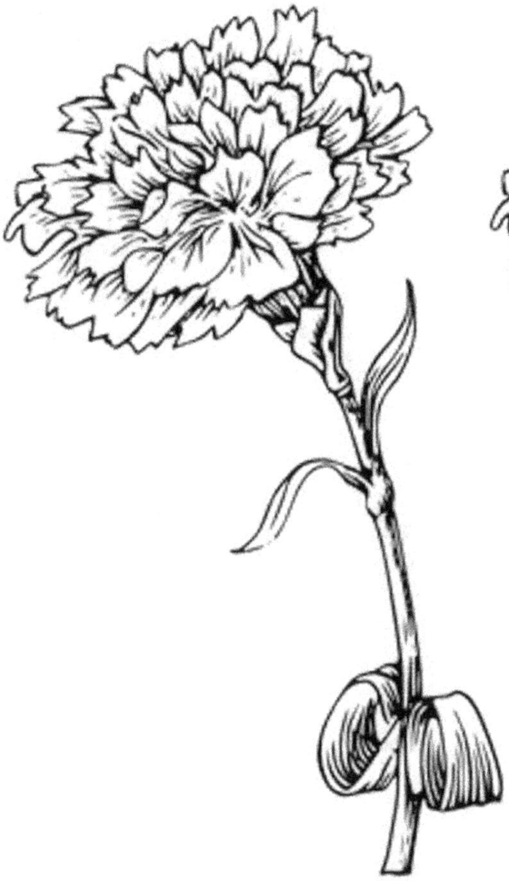
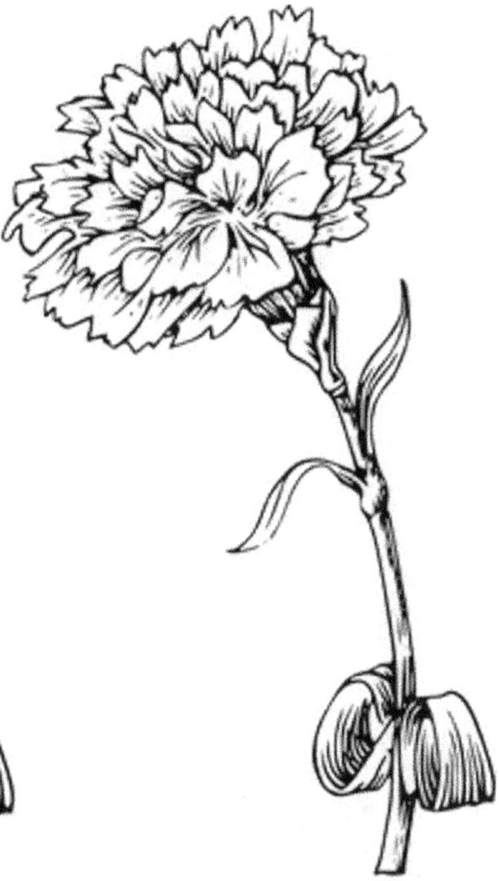
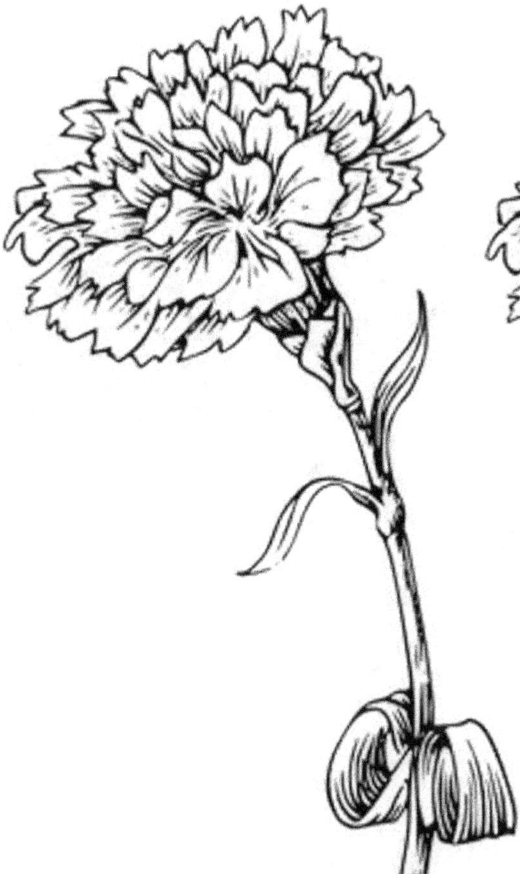
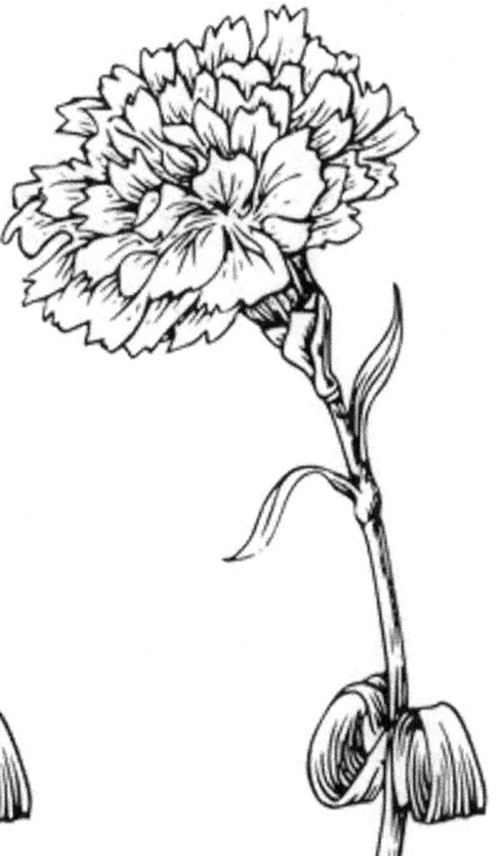

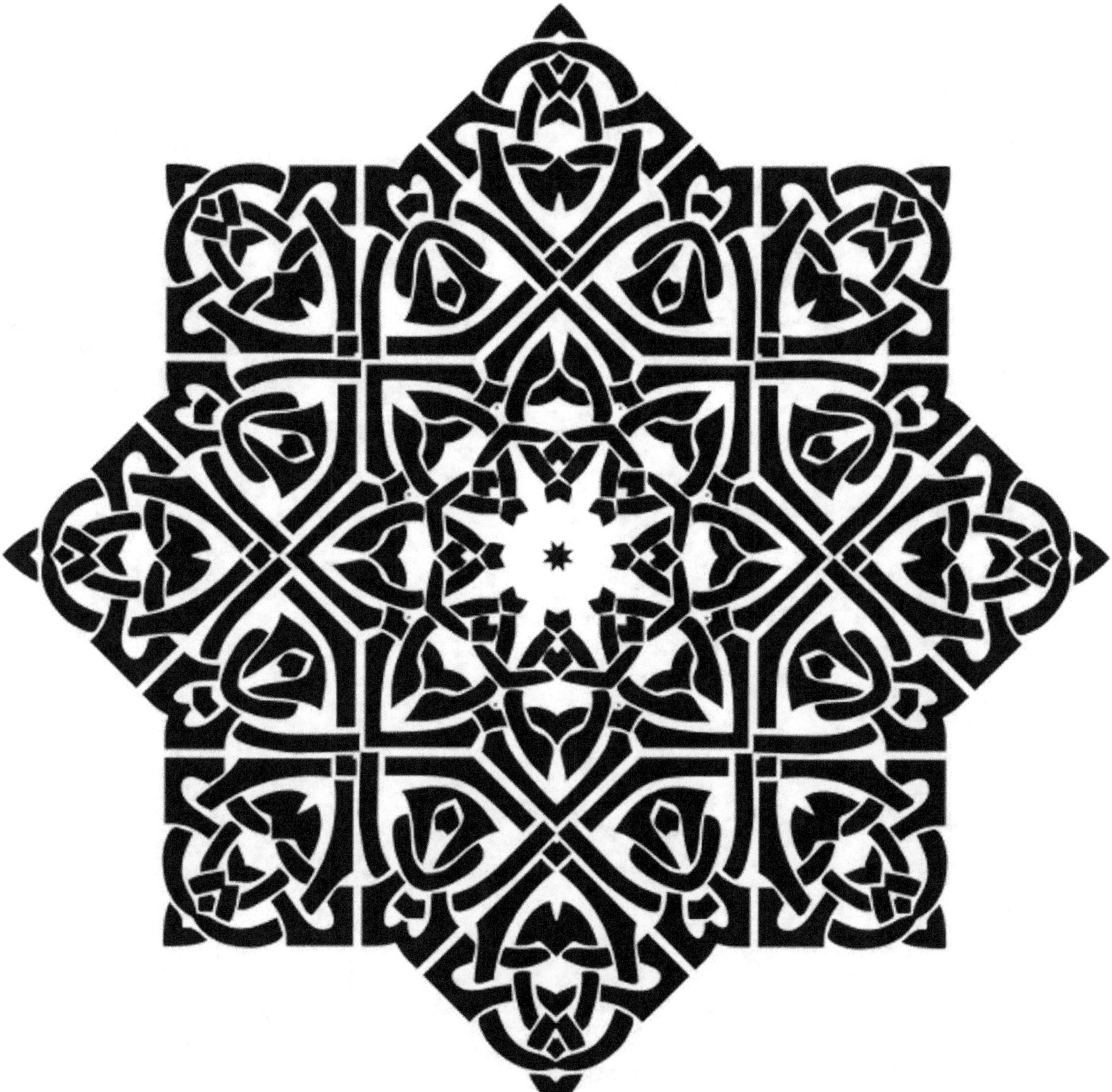

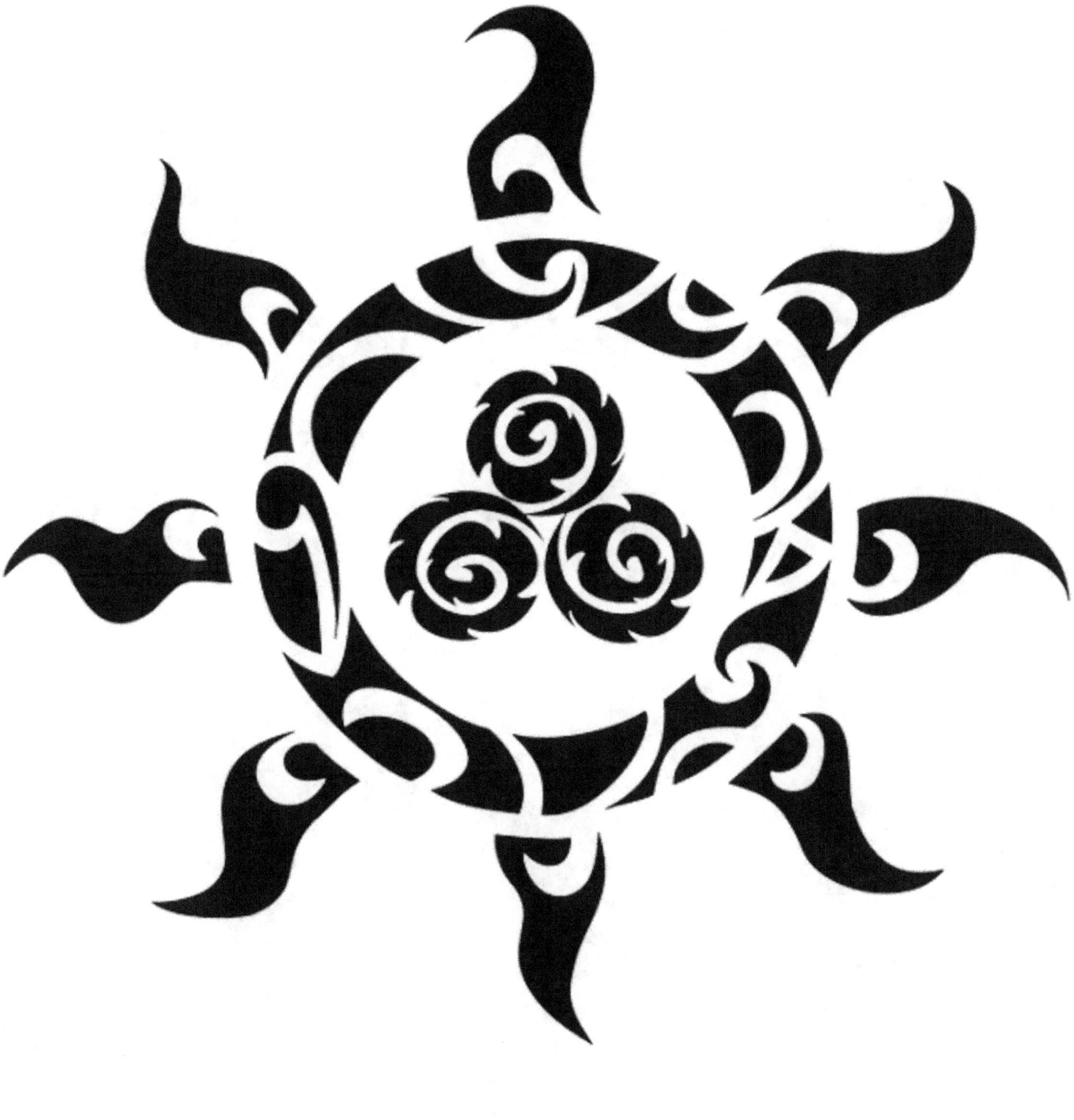

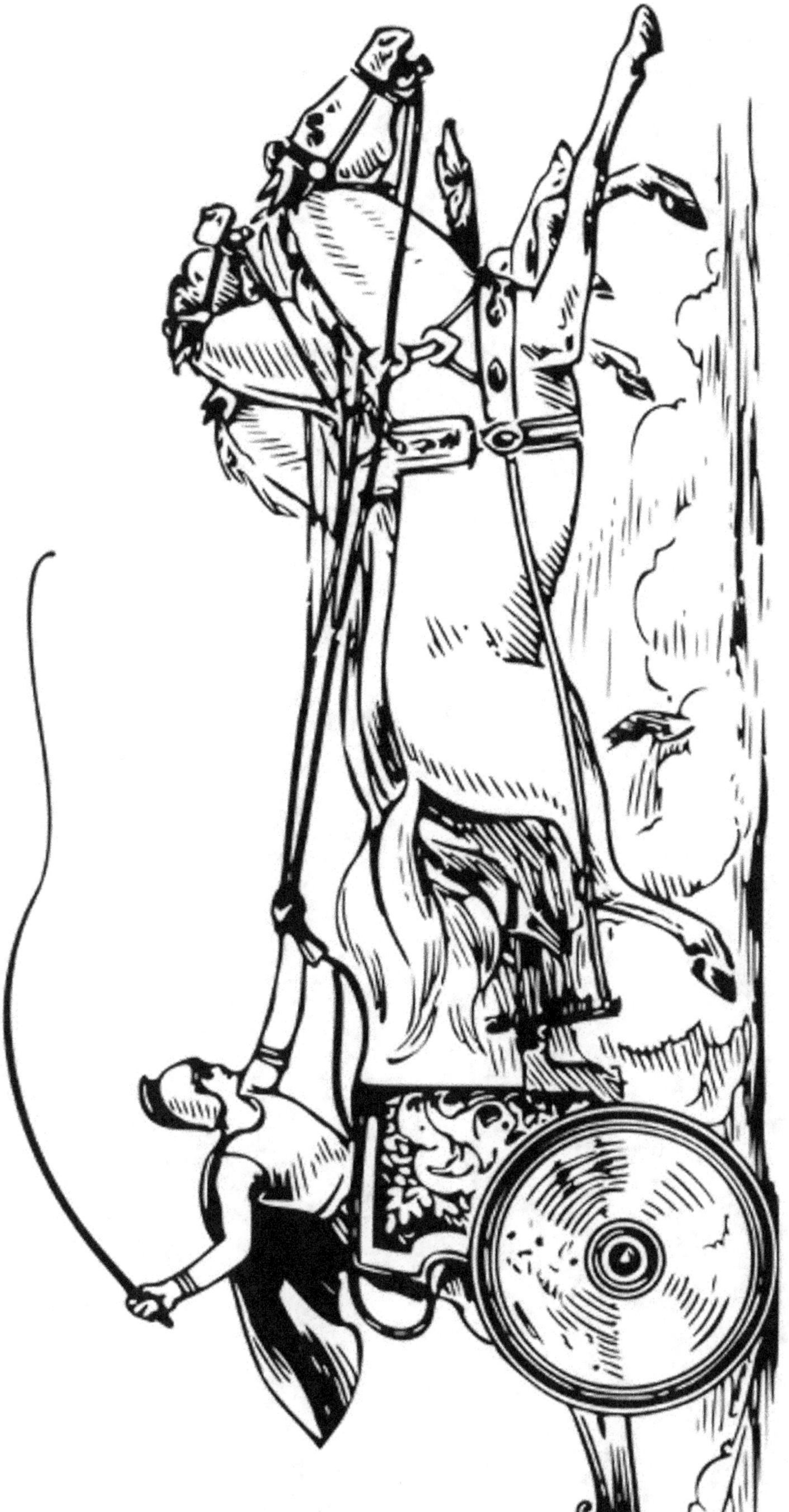

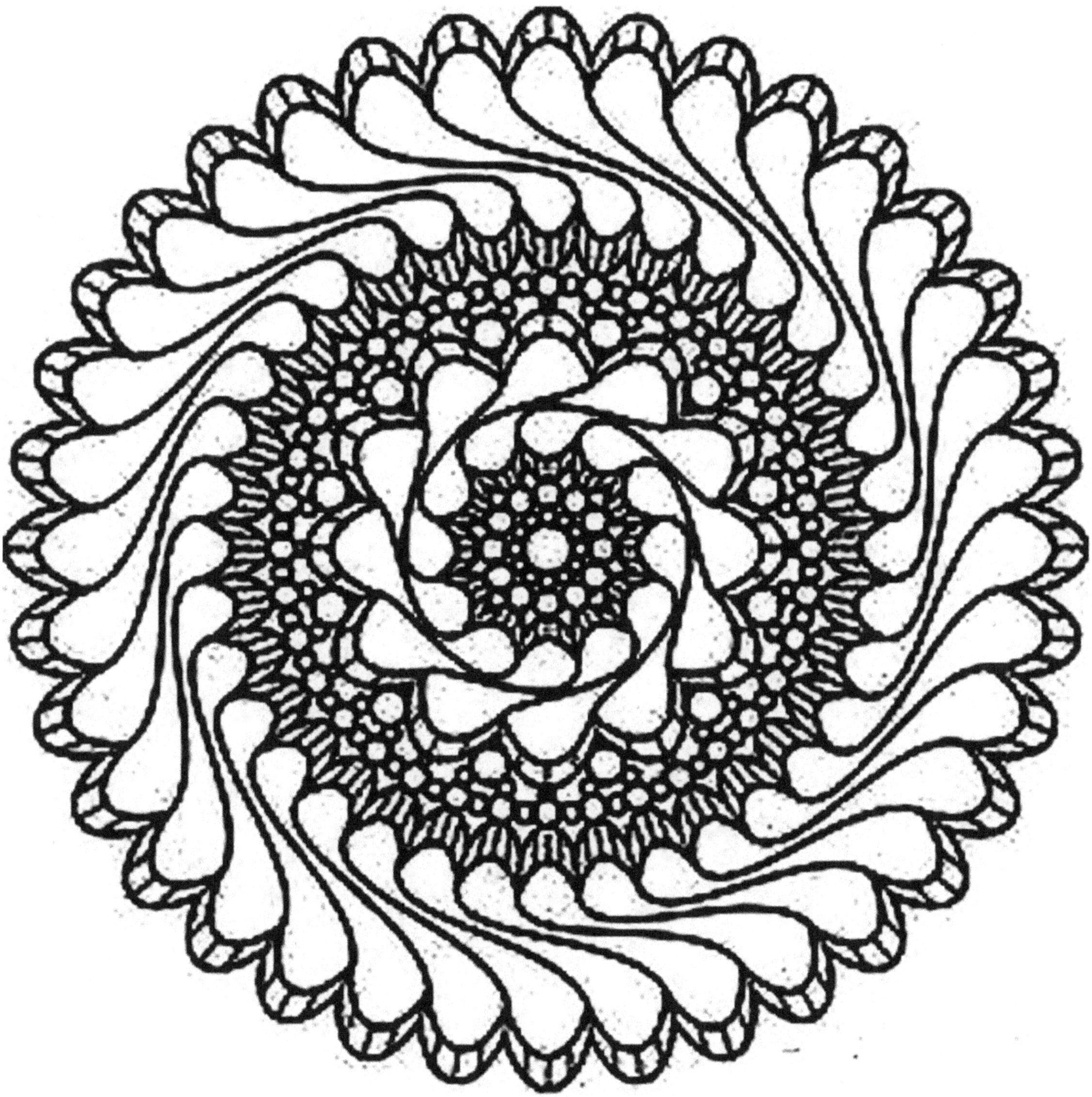

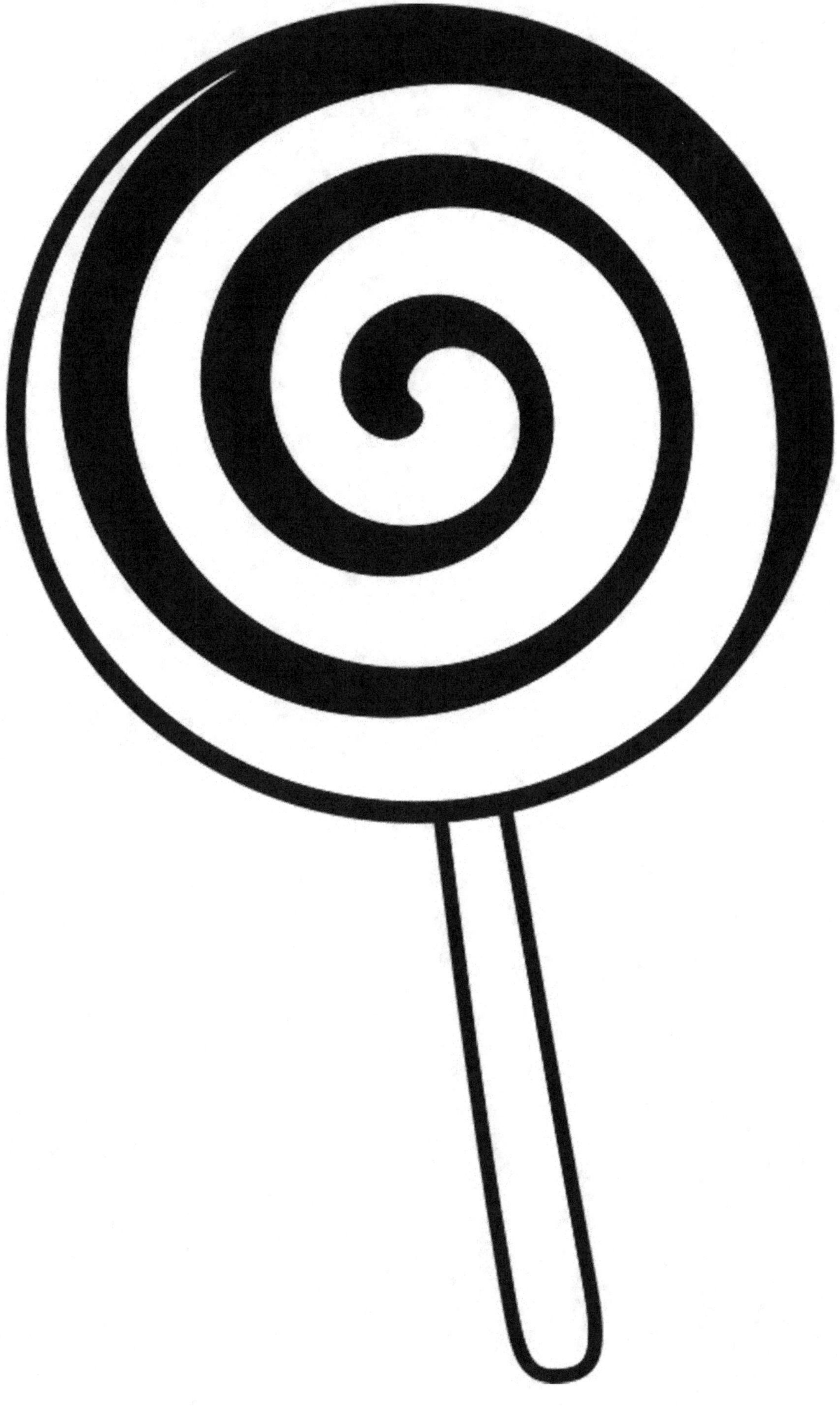

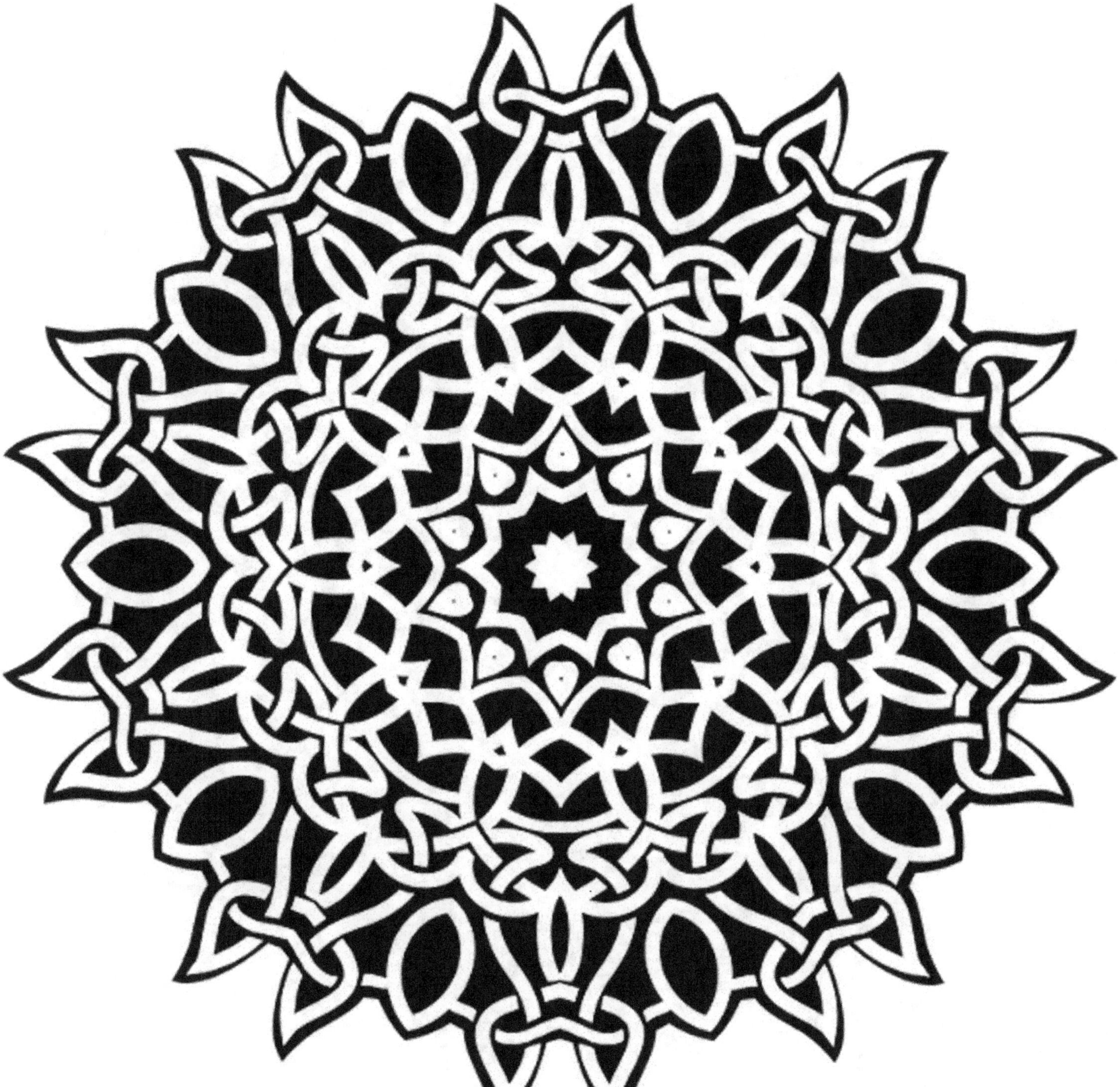

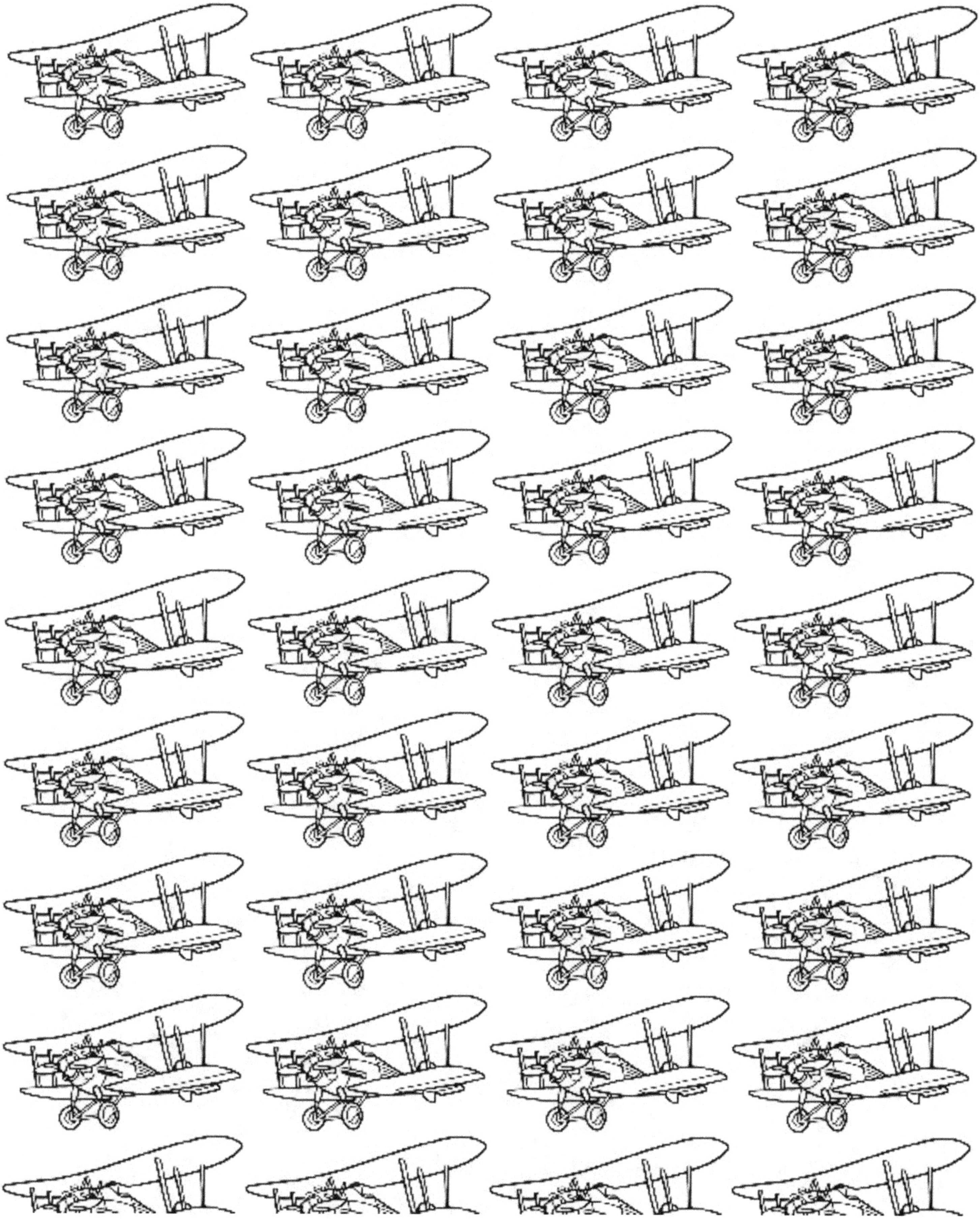

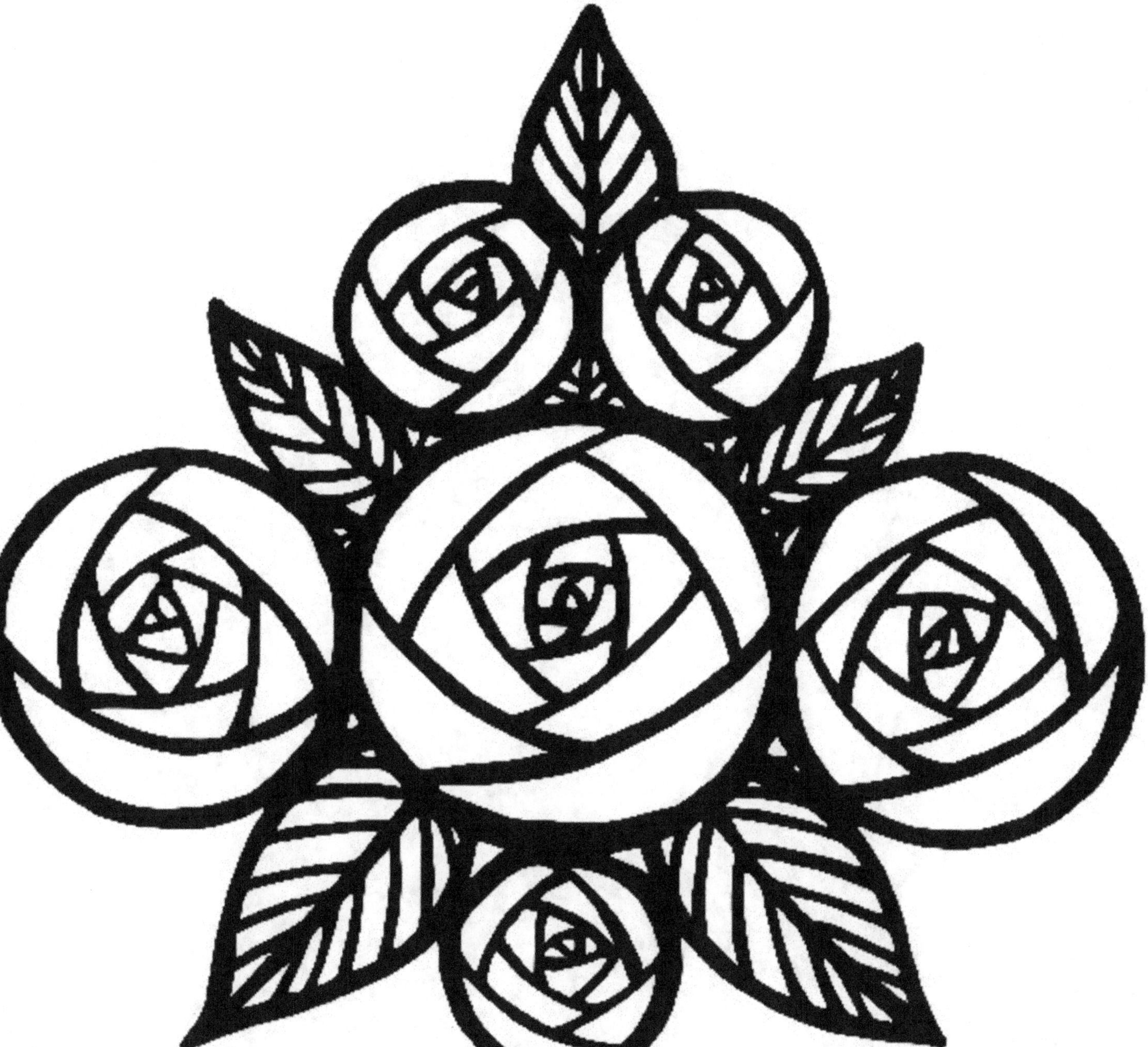

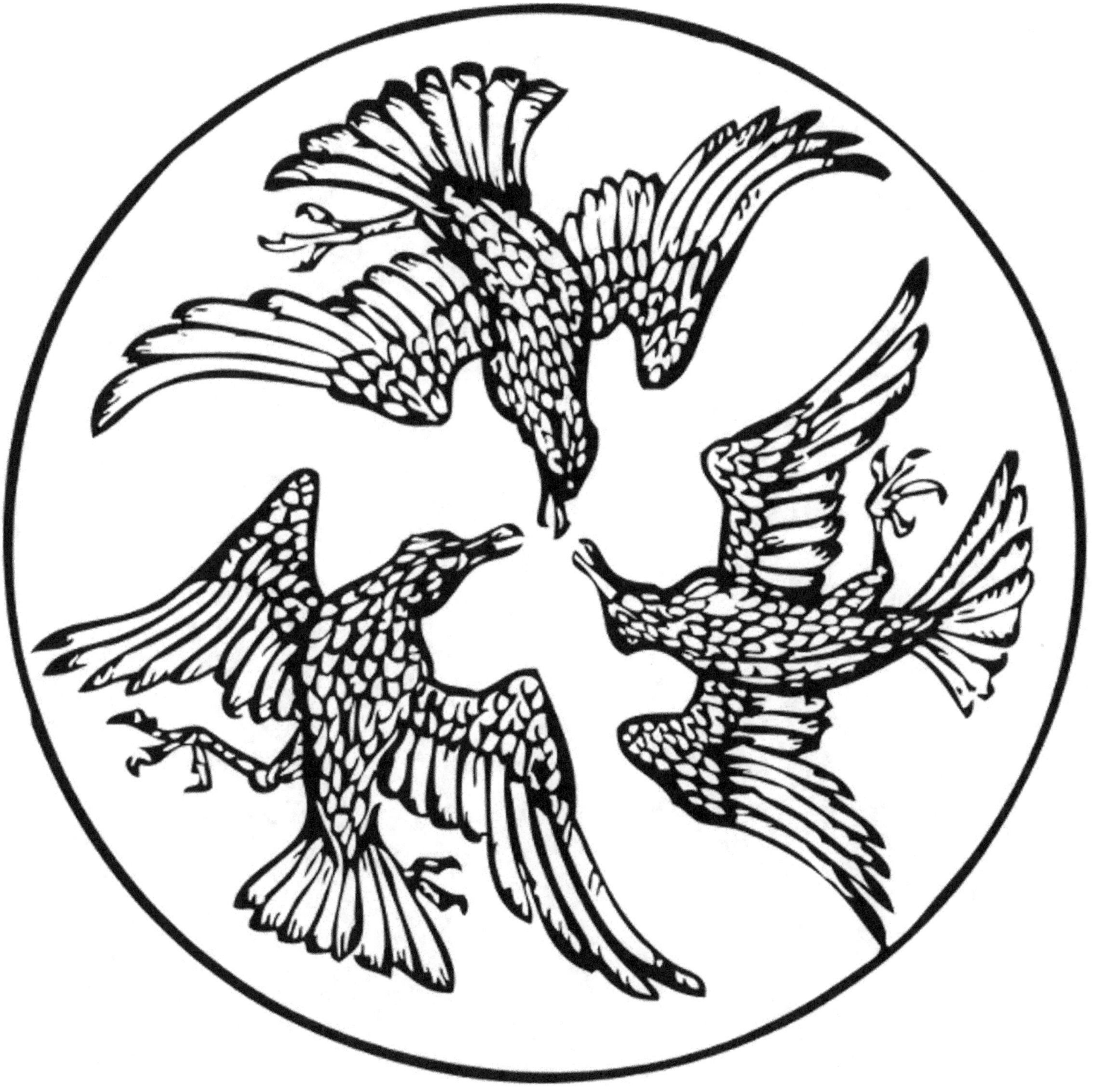

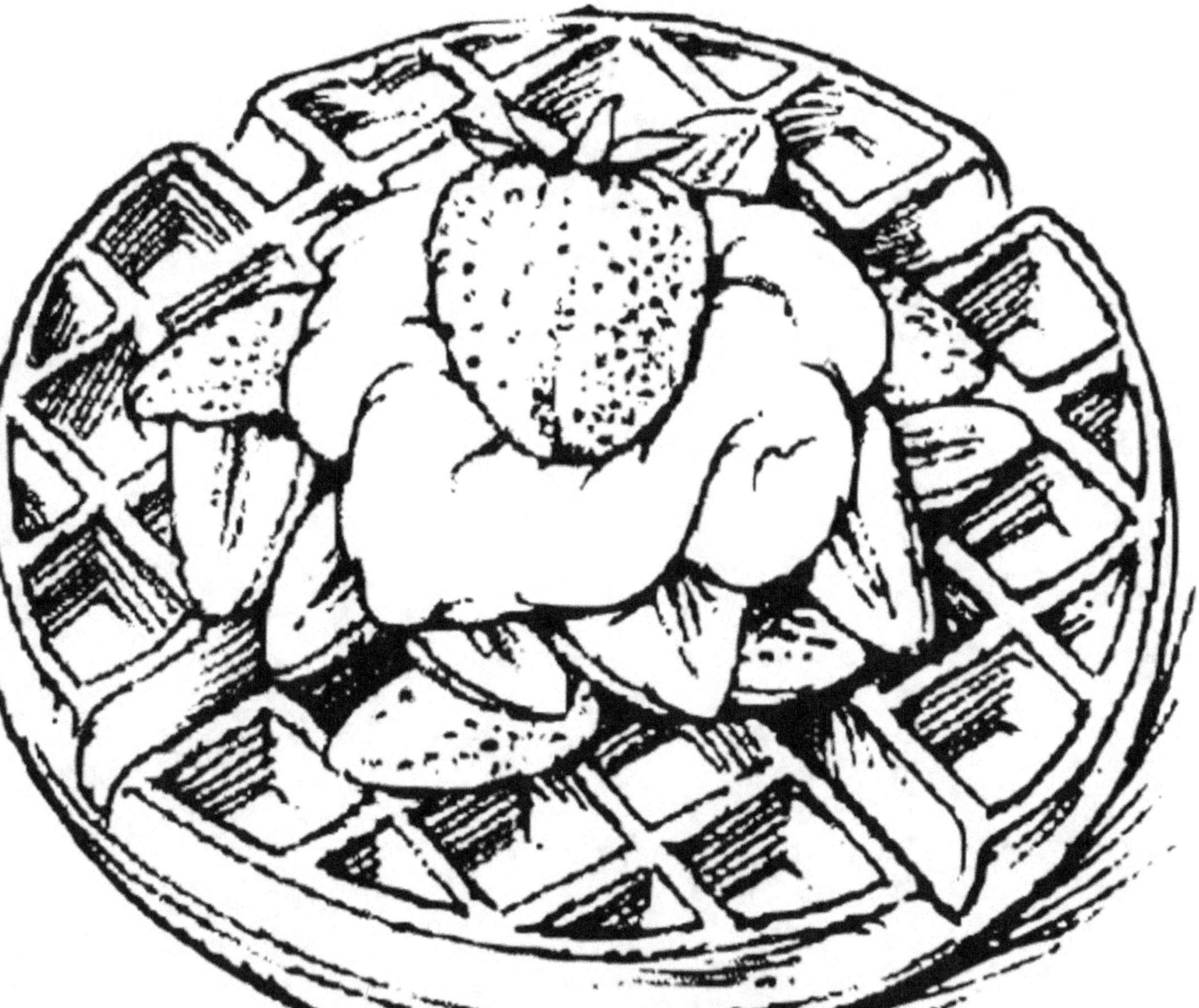

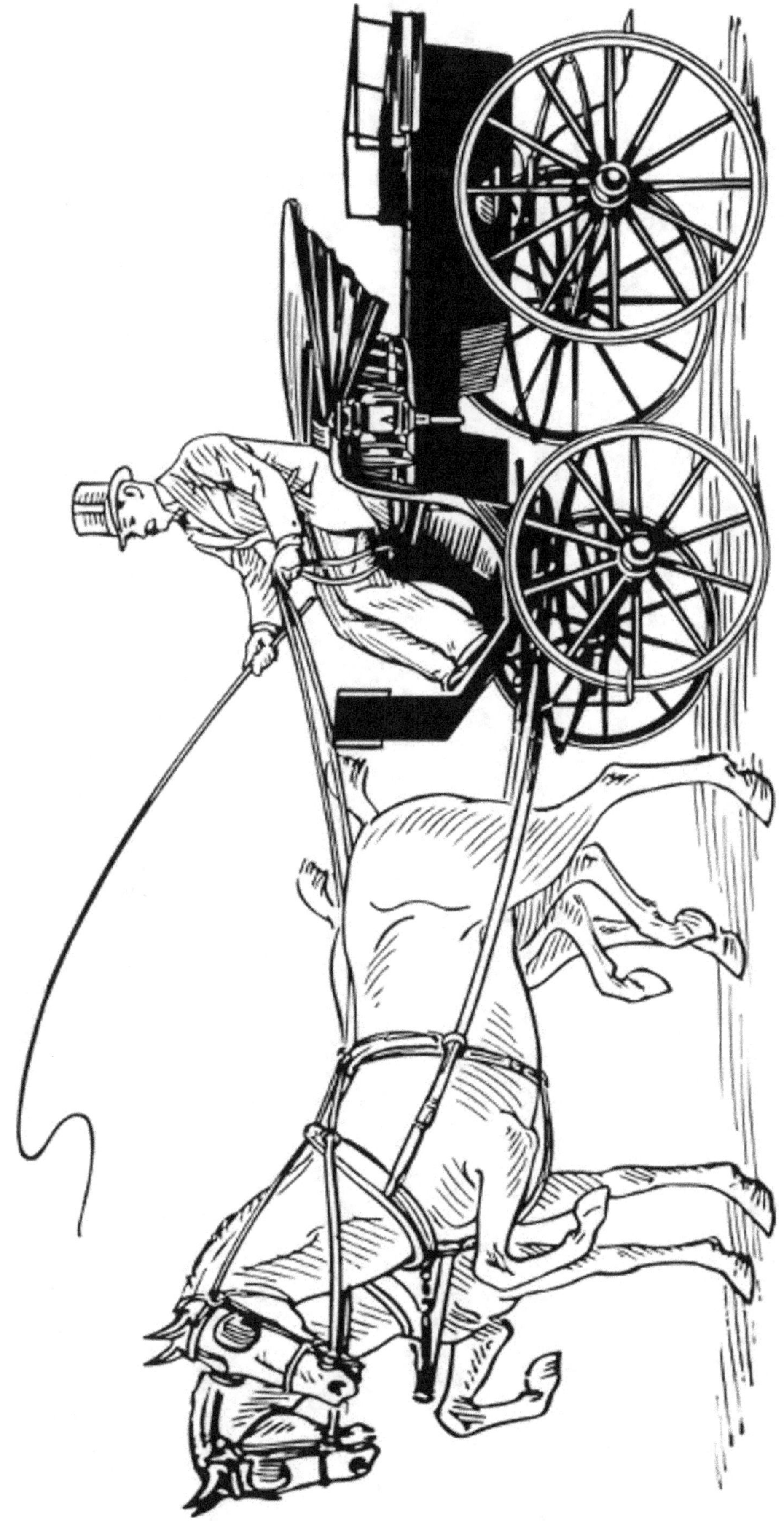

www.ingramcontent.com/pod-product-compliance
Lightning Source LLC
Chambersburg PA
CBHW081743220526
45468CB00008B/2220
* 9 7 8 1 7 9 2 6 6 5 8 9 9 *